The SS-Panzer-Artillery Regiment 1
Leibstandarte Adolf Hitler
(LAH)
1940-1945

Acknowledgments

My special thanks go to the artillery chronicler Horst Mutterlose for his decades of tireless work. Without his chronicle of the regiment, this book would not have been possible. His superb photos also supplied about half of the pictorial material. I thank all of those who supplied Mutterlose with photographs many years ago. Great thanks go to the soldiers of the 1st Battery, especially Erich Meyer, Richard Schrei and Reinhold Macke, for their cooperation. Kurt Frentrupp contributed much to this book with his diary notations and inclusive reports.

The late Karl Gross (+1999) and Eisse de Vries (+1998) supplied long and extremely precise combat reports. From my grandfather Wilhelm Auge (+1989) I received since 1984 not only photo albums, documents and tape recordings, but also some reminiscences. He deserves the highest recognition. Without him this book would never have existed. The late war correspondent Ernst Krause supplied drawings, photos and reports.

Contributions came from, among others, von Böttget, Busch, Dinter, Franke, Fritzsche, Gottzmann (+), Fork (+), Henssler, Ihle, Kandale (+), Kumm, Moll, Peckelsen, Pulvermüller, Rothe, Schlett (+), Hans Bernhard and Heinz Bernhardt.

LAH specialist Mr. Agte of Pluwig did much to complete the story, especially in the confirmation of decorations, promotions, positions held and death dates of certain soldiers.

Dipl. Ing. Werner Sunkel of the Military Technology Museum in Röthenbach on the Pegnitz (www.wehrtechnikmuseum.de) provided extensive technical information for the photos, I thank him heartily for all his help.

The Author

Photo Credits

Mutterlose Archives	127	Kurt Frentrup	8
Fischer Archives	23	Otto Kumm	1
Wilhelm Auge	14	Reinhold Macke	4
Hans Böttger	32	Erich Meyer	38
Erich Dinter	1	Richard Schrei	23

Documents, Sketches, Drawings

Mutterlose Archives	3
Fischer Archives	11

Bibliography

Die Leibstandarte, Vol. I-IV/2, by Rudolf Lehmann and Ralf Tiemann, Munin Verlag, Osnabrück.

Deutschland im Zweiten Weltkrieg, Vol. II-VI, by a group of authors under the direction of Wolfgang Schumann, Akademie-Verlag (DDR), Berlin.

Grenadiere von Panzermeyer, Schild-Verlag, Munich.

Unterrichtsbuch für Soldaten, Light Artillery (mot.) edition, by Hauptmann Weber, Verlag "Offene Worte," Berlin, W 35 (War edition 1939/1940).

Der lautlose Tod von Olaf Groehler, Verlag der Nation (DDR), Berlin.

Verbände und Truppen der deutschen Wehrmacht und Waffen-SS im 2. Weltkrieg, by G. Tessin, Verlag Mittler & Söhne, Frankfurt am Main.

Front cover illustration: The 5th Battery (Ost. Heberer) with the Reconaissance Unit of the Leibstandarte (Panzermeyer) at the Klisura Pass, Greece, April 14, 1941.

The Berta gun (Uscha. Oskar Speer) during a pause in firing.

The artillery chronicler Horst Mutterlose as a telephonist in ther medium construction troop, 2nd Battery/AR-LSSAH (12th Battery/AR-VT), after the end of the western campaign in July 1940.
Standing, from left to right: Muttelose, Peters (+), Pabst (+), Malina (+), Witzenhausen (driver of the intelligence unit's leader), seated, from left to right: Oberscharführer Fritz Vogel (Intelligence Unit, +); front: Walter Mück (+), Heinz Schütte (+), Walter Nofts (+).

The SS-Panzer-Artillery Regiment 1

Leibstandarte Adolf Hitler (LAH)

1940-1945

SS artillery in firing position, chalk drawing by war correspondent Ernst Krause of the SS Propaganda Company. The drawing shows a light howitzer of the 1st Battery in a firefight on the eastern front. War Correspondent Krause reported to the author:
"I knew Battery Chief Teufel well. His 1st Battery had attained success with the new light-measuring device. In the summer of 1941 I began to prepare drawings and reports for the press. I always had good relations with the Artillery Regiment. At Easter 1941 I experienced my baptism of fire with the guns at Kastoria Lake."
A contemporary original was saved through all the wartime and postwar times by Hauptscharführer Wilhelm Auge, then leader of the 1st Battery's intelligence unit. The author received it from him in September 1985. After 58 years I was able to give Ernst Krause a copy. All materials, including sketches, of this work had been lost in a bomb attack.

Thomas Fischer

Schiffer Military History
Atglen, PA

Translated from the German by Dr. Ed Force
Book Design by Ian Robertson.

Library of Congress Catalog Number: 2003112441

Printed in China.
ISBN: 0-7643-1982-5

This book was originally printed under the title,
Das SS-Panzer-Artillerie-Rgt. 1 LAH an allen Fronten 1940-1945 Eine Bildchronik
by Podzun Pallas Verlag

Published by Schiffer Publishing Ltd.
4880 Lower Valley Road
Atglen, PA 19310
Phone: (610) 593-1777
FAX: (610) 593-2002
E-mail: info@schifferbooks.com.
Visit our web site at: www.schifferbooks.com
Please write for a free catalog.
This book may be purchased from the publisher.
Please include $3.95 postage.
Try your bookstore first.

In Europe, Schiffer books are distributed by:
Bushwood Books
6 Marksbury Avenue
Kew Gardens
Surrey TW9 4JF
England
Phone: 44 (0) 20 8392-8585
FAX: 44 (0) 20 8392-9876
E-mail: info@bushwoodbooks.co.uk.
Free postage in the UK. Europe: air mail at cost.
Try your bookstore first.

Table of Contents

The resting column of the 2nd Battery in southern Ukraine, summer 1941—time for hygiene and a little nourishment.

Foreword

As the grandson of a longtime artilleryman of the Leibstandarte, I have been aware of the history of the troops since my childhood.

A short time after my grandfather's death in 1989, I was able to locate several of his comrades. A lively correspondence followed.

The idea of writing an artillery book grew out of the fact that no such account of their action is to be found on the market. Unfortunately, reports of the artillery regiment's sometimes spectacular actions are included only rarely in the history of the Leibstandarte division.

Between 1997 and 2001 I was able to turn up several photo albums with hitherto fully unknown pictures. Most of these photos had not seen the light of day since 1945; only eight had appeared in books since then. Some photos are faulty, since the amateur photographer often grabbed his camera in haste in the heat of battle. But because of their uniqueness, these photos were not eliminated.

Horst Mutterlose, as regimentyal chronicler, made extensive photographic material available. His chronicle served as the basis of this book and was completed with new information. The author has tried to amplify reports and add details from the experiences of other comrades. But since the experiences are almost six decades in the past, erroneous memories and descriptions of photos are possible.

It should be made clear to the reader that the role of the artillery had changed and gained importance during the course of the war.

The artilleryman, formerly satirized often as a "boom-boomer", who was safe behind the front, took part more and more often in direct firefight action with enemy tanks and massed infantry. The artillery suffered from constant demands: supporting its own infantry in attack and defense, eliminating enemy artillery, breaking up positions, fighting off tanks and fulfilling tasks required by superior command offices—the demands were heavy. And the LASH artillery was always with the division at the focal points of the combat. The Leibstandarte, and especially its light batteries (1st-3rd) as its senior artillery units, took part in all the important battles of World War II. Sometimes they were with the most advanced units, farthest into enemy territory.

Necessary for lasting success of artillery tasks were sufficient ammunition and fast movement of supplies. Chronic shortages of artillery shells and often-broken supply lines sometimes limited their firepower, which did not earn that service arm greater popularity.

German ammunition production suffered, as in World War I, from a shortage of explosives. The main cause was the constant lack of nitrogen, which was accepted by the Blitzkrieg strategists as part of the situation. The ammunition shortage became more and more of a problem during the war.

May this book contribute to a greater appreciation of the artillerymen.

Thomas Fischer
Berlin, Autumn 2002

The author and chronicler with his grandfather, Wilhelm Auge, the reporter of the 1st Battery, at the 750-year celebration in Berlin. The photo was taken in the newly rebuilt Nikolai district of central Berlin in July 1987.

Swearing in the young artillerymen of the II./SS Artillery Replacement Unit at the LSSAH barracks in Berlin-Lichterfelde on December 21, 1939. The men did not know that only four months later they would belong to the SS Leibstandarte Adolf Hitler Division.

Establishment of the LSSAH Artillery Regiment and Origin of the Batteries

The Artillery Regiment was established by order of August 19, 1940 as to the strengthening of the Leibstandarte SS Adolf Hitler unit. It originated from the SS Artillery Regiment of the SS Reserve Troop. Obersturmbannführer Peter Hansen, as of June 1, 1939, was to form the first artillery unit of the SS-VT at the training camp in Jüterbog. Within eight weeks a fully field-ready regiment had been created through day and night training. Sharpshooting took place almost every day.

At first the three light units were set up with nine batteries. In the II./SS-AR-VT led by Sturmbannführer Hermann Priess (ultimately Commanding General of the 1st SS Armored Corps) was the 5th Battery. This unit is of special interest for the further history of the LAH artillery, as it later became the 1st Battery/AR-Leibstandarte SS Adolf Hitler. It will be mentioned often. As the oldest LAH battery, it was often at the focal points of battles. In March 1940 the IV. Unit/SS-AR-VT, likewise a light unit, was formed. It consisted of the young recruits (see photo) who joined the II. SS Artillery Replacement Unit in Berlin-Lichterfelde on November 30, 1939. In mid-January 1940 it was transferred to Munich-Freimann and found a new home in the barracks of the SS "Deutschland" Regiment.

In April 1940 the IV. Unit of the SS Artillery Regiment of the SS Reserve Troop was tactically assigned to the Leibstandarte SS Adolf Hitler. SS Obergruppenführer Sepp Dietrich, Commander of the LSSAH, added the Artillery Unit organiocally to his strengthened regiment. Quarters were occupied in Rheine, Westphalia. On Tuesday, April 16, 1940, the Commander of the SS-AR-VT, Peter Hansen, reviewed the unit commanded by Sturmbannführer Walter Staudinger. At the beginning of the western campaign on May 9, 1940 the Unit received its "Adolf Hitler" sleeve stripe. The batteries (10, 11, 12) remained in the LSSAH until the war ended.

When the western campaign began, a heavy artillery unit with 15-cm howitzers was formed for the SS Reserve Troop. The V. (heavy) Unit/SS-AR-VT (Batteries 13-15) thus came into being. On August 20, 1940, both the 5th Battery/SS-AR-VT and the 14th (heavy) Battery under Obersturmbannführer Heberer were completely transferred to the Leibstandarte. The SS-AR-LSSAH that now originated from the first SS Artillery Regiment consisted not only of a light unit with three batteries but also of a heavy unit with two batteries of 15-cm sFH 18 and one 8.8-cm Flak battery.

A diagram of the close-knit unity of the SS-AR-VT and SS-AR-LSSAH regiments will make the situation clearer to the reader.

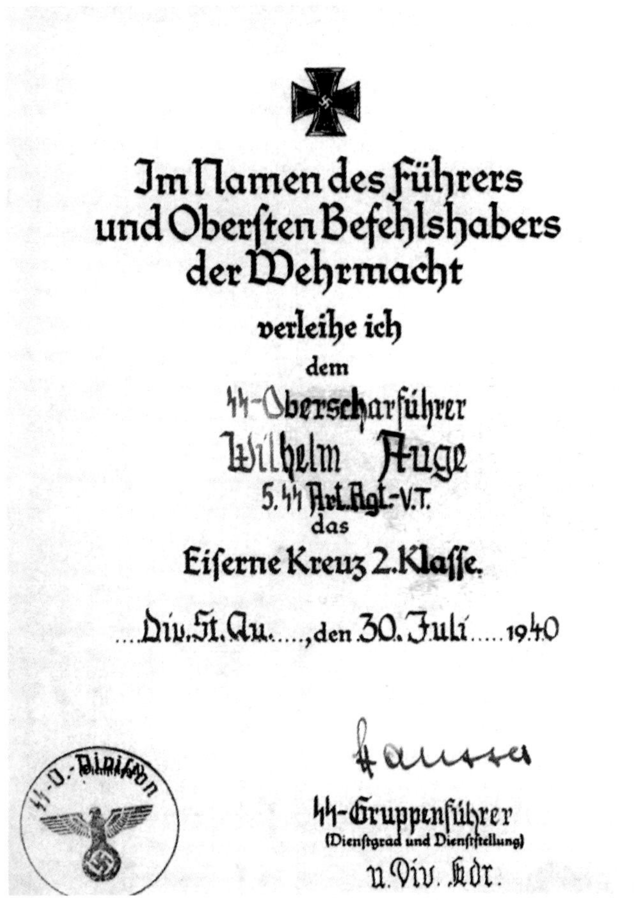
Im Namen des Führers
und Obersten Befehlshabers
der Wehrmacht
verleihe ich
dem
SS-Oberscharführer
Wilhelm Auge
5. SS Art.Rgt.-V.T.
das
Eiserne Kreuz 2. Klasse.
...Div.St.Qu....., den 30. Juli 1940
SS-Gruppenführer
(Dienstgrad und Dienststellung)
u. Div. Kdr.

The 5th Battery of the VT Artillery Regiment belonged to the newly-formed SS-V-Division. Its commander was the Inspector of the SS Reserve Troop, SS Gruppenführer Paul Hausser. By his soldiers he was always called "Papä Hausser.

Das erste SS-Artillerie-Regiment der SS-Verfügungstruppe und Abgabe von Batterien an die Leibstandarte SS Adolf Hitler

SS-Artillerie-Regiment-VT (später SS-Art.Rgt. "Das Reich" bzw.
SS-Panzer-Artillerie-Regiment 2 "Das Reich")

I.Abteilung

1.Batterie
2.Batterie
3.Batterie

II.Abteilung

4.Batterie
5.Batterie (Hst.v.Saucken, ab Mai 1940
6.Batterie Ost.Drexler)

20.8.1940

III.Abteilung

7.Batterie
8.Batterie
9.Batterie
--------------vor dem Polenfeldzug

IV.Abteilung

ab 12.4.1940 der LAH im Einsatz unterstellt

10.Batterie (Hst.Sukkau)
11.Batterie (Ost.Schröder)
12.Batterie (Ost.Cischek)
--------------vor dem Westfeldzug

V.Abteilung

13.Batterie
14.Batterie (Ost.Heberer) — 20.8.1940
15.Batterie
--------------mit dem Westfeldzug einsatzbereit

Aufstellung der ersten-dritten Abteilung mit Wirkung vom 1.Juni 1939

Aufstellung der vierten Abteilung im März 1940

Aufstellung der fünften Abteilung ab April 1940

SS-Artillerie-Regiment-LSSAH
(später SS-Panzer-Artillerie-Rgt.1 "Leibstandarte SS Adolf Hitler")

I.Abteilung (Stubaf.Sukkau)

1.Batterie (Ost.Teufel)
2.Batterie (Hst.Cischek)
3.Batterie (Ost.Horns)

II.Abteilung (Stubaf.Mertsch)

4.Batterie (Hst.Schröder)
5.Batterie (Ost.Heberer)
6.Batterie (Ost.Fend)
Diese 8,8-cm-Flakbatterie kam ab Anfang Oktober von der Flakschule Rerik.

Aufstellung mit Wirkung vom 19.August 1940,

weiterer Ausbau ab Mai 1941

The 5th Battery AR/VT in the Western Campaign of 1940

In firing position: light Howitzer 18 after firing!
The gun was put into position quickly and has opened fire. The muzzle cap and covering cloth were simply lowered and still hang on the gun. The 5th Battery was subordinate to the SS Infantry Regiment "Der Führer."

Heavy fighting rages along the Grebbe Line in Holland, and as of June 1940 on the Avre and Sommer Front (penetration battle near Arras).
Beside the guns, explosive shells with Impact Fuse 23 and cartridge baskets for six cartridges lie ready. The battery fired at its fastest rate of fire and scattered fog shells to impede the enemy's sight.

Above: *For camouflage reasons, the SS-VT wore no SS lapels in the western campaign. In the field mail, Wehrmacht ranks were used by senders and recipients (for example, Wachtmeister instead of SS Oberscharführer). These two junior officers belong to the ammunition staff. In the background are "Uniform Diesel" (right) and Mercedes LG 3000 (left) trucks.* Below: *The first battery chief of the 5th SS-AR-VT was Hauptsturmführer Harald von Saucken, son of Armored General and 27th Knight's Cross Diamond wearer Dietrich von Saucken (in camouflage jacket). The battery officer was Ernst Roentsch (center).*

Attention! Low-flying planes! Anti-aircraft defense is provided from an AA truck (Kfz. 4) by Sturmmann Wolfert.

Above: *The advance pauses in La Bassee. The car of the battery chief, Obersturmführer Drexler, is surrounded by his men. The Observation Officer, Ust. Herbert Nix (leaning on the fender) and the Intelligence Unit Leader, Oscha. Wilhelm Auge (in the background with binoculars), can be recognized by their peaked caps. Oskar Drexler commanded the SS Armored Artillery Regiment 12 "Hitler Youth" from the summer of 1944 to the war's end and received the Knight's Cross.* Below: *Two captured French "Chenilette" infantry tractors with trailers are examined by Unterscharführer Rolf Lentz to the right of the advance column of the 5th Battery. Some 6200 of this type were built in all. The "Lorraine Tractor" was used by the French Army since 1931.*

A firing position on the Bay of Biscay (Biarritz) after the western campaign ended. The march of the SS V Division ended at the Spanish border.

After the fighting ended, an inclusive maintenance of weapons and equipment took place. Franz Müntzel (front, polishing a boot) later became a marksman in the first days at the Rollbahn Nord (July 1941) and shot down the first Russian tank with the lFH 18 howitzer. On August 20, 1940 the 5th Battery was transferred to the Leibstandarte. Rudolf Fritzsche brought five factory-new tractors to Metz from the Army Supply Depot at Güstrow.

The IV. AR-VT with the Leibstandarte in the Western Campaign in 1940

Above: *The head of a unit crossed the Netherlands border on the Bentheim-Oldenzaal road on May 10, 1940. An unusual rig: During the entire campaign all twelve light howitzers were towed by infantry Schützenpanzerwagen (SPW)!* Below: *Motorcycles of the unit staff on the road toward Ijssel on May 11, 1940. On May 13, 1940 it passed through Ijsselburg and on to Rees.*

May 14, 1940: Attack on Rotterdam. The Luftwaffe bomb attacks could no longer be stopped, though they also endangered the Leibstandarte, already located on the north quay of the harbor peninsula. Several bombs struck before and behind the artillery's position. In the evening hours the IV. Unit drove through burning Rotterdam after its surrender. In the further course of the western campaign the unit passed through Clermont-Ferrand to St. Etienne. In the period from May 10 to June 24 the LSSAH was subordinated to 26 different command offices.

Officers of the IV. Unit at the ossuary of the Douaumont cemetery on July 28, 1940. Hauptsturmführer Sukkau (center, with Käppi) stood out during the western campaign by his outstanding fire control and effective action. On May 27 he was wounded with the infantry's spearhead, and he was the first artilleryman to receive the Iron Cross I on Jule 7, 1940. The German losses were not insubstantial. One of many examples: On June 6, 1940 the Artillery Survey Regiment (AVT Staff) hit a mine. There were four fatalities (Heblich, Groschner, Mommert, Kröger) and one badly wounded man (Beigel).

Above - *Autumn 1940: Obergruppenführer Sepp Dietrich with leaders and commanders od the Artillery Regiment. Sturmbannführer Gustav Mertsch (5th from left) took over the I. Unit. The mighty 8-ton tractors for the heavy howitzers are in the rear.* Below: *The 5th (sFH) Battery, formerly 14./SS-AR-VT, is seen in Metz-Frescaty after being transferred to the Leibstandarte. Gun cleaning is stil being done in white drill uniforms.*

1

The Balkan Campaign 1941

Because of the Italian offensive against Egypt, preparations were made to take possession of the Greek mainland north of the Aegean Islands from Bulgaria, if necessary, and to create the prerequisites for the use of German air units against targets on the eastern Mediterranean. In particular, these measures were aimed at the British support points which threatened the Romanian oil fields. This area was vitally important for the German war effort. The German worries were intensified in military terms by the Italian advance on Greece from Albania. It allowed the British to make military use of Greece. For that reason the advance command of the Leibstandarte, under Obersturmbannführer Staudinger, set out for Romania as early as January 14, 1941, in order to prepare quarters for the division in the Constanza-Tulcea area. The quarters were never occupied. The advance command transferred to Tulcea for reasons of security, in order to protect the area of the south arm of the Danube from the north. Only in mid-March 1941 did the units of the LSSAH arrive at the southern edge of the Transylvanian Alps. Then the Leibstandarte headed for Bulgaria. It was subordinated to the XXXX. Army Corps under General of the Cavalry Stumme. The development of the situation in Belgrade—a revolt removed the old government—then led to a hostile attitude in Yugoslavia and an attack.

Before the departure to the Balkans, a light troop anti-aircraft truck (Kfz. 4, made by BMW) is secured on a flatcar. A twin mount held two MG 34 guns.

Above: Wilhelm Auge (center) of the 1st Battery and the intelligence unit were already in the Tulcea area with the advance command as of January 1941. Below: From March 5 to 8, 1941, 28 transport trains left Metz. The Leibstandarte was sent to the AOK 12 (List). Here Fritz Schröder (2nd from left) and his 4th Battery are shown during a stop at a Hungarian depot.

The gun unit of the 1st Battery takes a break in Romania. The rear of the towing tractor has a full load of gasoline canisters. The driver of the Hopfner gun's tractor was Rottenführer Fritzsche.

The battery chief of the 3./Artillery Regiment LAH, Hinrich Horns, stands before a 3-ton towing tractor in Romania. Obersturmführer Horns was badly wounded in the first days in Russia. By chance, Obergruppenführer Dietrich passed by the dying battery chief in the Leibstandarte's field hospital. He immediately promoted him to Hauptsturmführer. Miraculously, Horns did not succumb to his abdominal wound, and by the war's end he was an Obersturmbannführer and Commander of the "Nibelungen" Artillery Regiment.

The regimental commander, Standartenführer Walter Staudinger, is greeted warmly by the local population.

April 6, 1941 was chosen as X-Day. Obergruppenführer Sepp Dietrich discussed the coming action with Unit Commander Sukkau (right). The2nd Battery was subordinated to the II. Battalion. On a reconnaissance trip, the Battery Chief, Hst. Cischek, and Sturmbannführer Mohnke (the Battalion Commander), were badly wounded by Yugoslavian bombs in Kuestendil. That necessitated a change in command for the regiment.

The Witt Battalion then assumed the leading position. April 7, 1941 was spent waiting. On April 8 the Yugoslavian border was crossed. The LAH followed the Army's 9th Armored Division.

Obersturmführer Fritz Teufel, Battery Chief of the 1./SS-AR "LSSAH," is seen before the march to the scene of action.

On April 8, 1941 they marched into Serbia. All four of the First Battery's guns have lined up here. The breakthrough into southern Serbia led through Kumanovo, Prilop and Bitoly and on to the Greek border near Niki on April 10.

The Battle for the Klidi Pass

After the LSSAH had crossed the Greek border near Niki in the morning hours of April 10, 1941, they reached the area around Florina, Lofi and Vevi later on the same day. The entire approach area lay below the dominating heights on both sides of Klidi. The coverless terrain allowed movement only in the prevailing stormy weather, with snow, rain and limited visibility. The Witt Battle Group was to push forward over the pass. All available artillery was to support the attack. But heavy snow robbed the artillery of any possibility of observation and effect, so that the attack was postponed to April 12, 1941. At 9:00 A.M. the 1st Company (Pleiss) moved out, and by noon it had taken possession of the heights.

Sturmmann Karl-Friedrich Meyer of the 5th (sFH) Battery reported on the combat for the Klidi Pass: "It began to get dark when we left the Florina area behind us and approached the mountains in the direction of the Klidi Pass. We slogged forward over a boggy field path and took up a position on the slope of a chain of hills. Within sight of us, the 4th Battery went into position to our left and the Flak unit to our right. Thus the entire heavy unit of the Leibstandarte was united for major action for the first time. The positions had been derived on the basis of aiming procedures, and the heavy field howitzers with their aiming mechanisms were placed in their positions, which were marked with wooden blocks. We had already laid down rush mats for the gun wheels, because of the soft ground. Then the tractors were uncoupled.

Now the cannoneers' routine work began.

The barrels were unbolted and moved forward, the limbers removed, the spars spread and the spurs set into the ground to take up the recoil. Each Cannoneer 1 (K1) set up the optical aiming device and used the built-in water level to set it vertically, with the traverse gauge at zero. The K3s ran to the rear with the red and white swabs and were positioned by the K1s via the optics. When the settings were right, the markers were rammed into the ground. Thus the groundwork for firing was completed. The other man unloaded the ammunition carriers. Shells and cartridge cases were stacked up behind the guns. The empty ammunition trucks drove right back to a depot in the rear to load up again. We were ready to fire! Two MG 34 guns on tripods were at hand for anti-aircraft defense.

With our "Ready to fire!" the enemy's heavy artilery also began to fire on our area with its heavy gun batteries. We were grateful for our protected position, for the trajectories of their shells could not reach us. They struck a good hundred meters behind our position.

And then we cut loose: "Command to fire!"—the second gun had, as usual, begun to home in. Then the whole battery opened up with effective fire. The 4th Battery followed, and the 8.8 Flak gun also took an indirect part in the ground combat as an ordinary rapid-fire cannon battery.We fired varying cartridge loads at various distances—on average, about 10 kilometers, but with greater charges up to about 13 km. It was very hard physical work that went on until it grew dark. Only during the night did the field kitchen come forward, as driving the nearby roads was almost impossible on account of the enemy's steady fire."

On the morning of the next day (6:30 A.M.) twelve British tanks attached southeast of the advance route west of Lakka, under heavy artillery cover. As the pass road was not yet completely cleared, there was only one light antitank gun ahead, which was hit at once. The chief of the 8.8 Flak battery (6./AR-LSSAH), who had arrived just west of Klidi, immediately came over the ridge to move his guns forward. At the top of the pass he was stopped by Commanding General Stumme, who said it was insane to [p. 27] take on a tank attack with such limited means. After he had persuaded him to get the best information on the situation (Fend had been freed from captivity), Stumme let him drive on, shaking his head. There Dr. Naumann was waiting to position the guns.

Vevi, April 11, 1941: Sepp Dietrich outlines the action with Battalion Commander Witt of the I./LSSAH and the leader of the subordinated 5th Battery (Ost. Heberer, right).

Above: *Turbulent weather before the storm on the Klidi Pass: Radioman Knapp (1st Battery) keeps in touch.* Below: *Oberscharführer Wilhelm Auge, Intelligence Unit Leader of the 1st Battery, with his men after the Klidi Pass was taken.*

He reported: "Taking a position was rarely so exciting. While the tanks rolled ahead, our guns opened fire directly from the heights of hte pass. Within a few minutes, eight tanks were already his and burning. The others avoided the direct fire and draw back behind the heights." With that the situation was cleaned out. Sepp Dietrich congratulated the Flak men in their position on their great success.

The opening of the Klidi Pass, the gate to the heart of Greece, placed the key to the successful conclusion of the campaign in our hands.

On April 14, 1942 the reconnaissance unit's attack on the Klisura Pass was continued. Panzermeyer had not only the 8.8 cm Flak guns but also Dr. Naumann's heavy howitzers at his disposal. But Battery Chief Heberer had to report to the commander of the Reconnaissance Unit that he could not support the attack without endangering the attacking companies. The guns were in firing positions, one after another, on the mountain road. But the road was so narrow that they had to be fired without spurs. Heberer declined any responsibility.

The impatient Panzermeyer ordered fire to be opened. It had to be done. Gurgling, the heavy 15-cm. shells flew over the first ridge and shattered the enemy positions to the left and right of the small mountain village.

How things went for the 5th Battery was reported by Cannoneer Meyer of the 2nd gun: "The battery is limited by a sight-obscuring right bend of the road. Only the second gun under Uscha. Speer was quickly advanced around the bend. An impressive, clear view of the enemy unfolded before our astonished eyes. Lit by the sun, the valley that led toward Kastoria lay before us between the 2000-meter height of the Vermon mountains. After quick routine work, the heavy howitzer was ready to fire. The earth spurs were thrown aside because the rocky material of the road did not allow their use. Meanwhile the ammunition was unloaded and the first shot was fired. The Greeks fled down the slope of the pass road.

"Now one explosive shell after another flew out of the barrel at targets up to 7 km away. The battery officer, Untersturmführer Luhmann, has his binoculars constantly before his eyes. Standing next to the gun, he continually calls out the corrections. Unmfortunately, the terrain allows only our gun to be fired. After the barrel becomes hot and a lot of ammunition is used, the welcome order to cease fire comes."

Panzermeyer reported in his book "Grenadiere": "What nobody would have thought possible, and is still regarded as madness

Sturmbannführer Fritz Witt (2nd from right) confers with the Commander of the 9th Panzer Division of the Army, Dr. Alfred Ritter von Hubicki (3rd from right).

today, my grenadiers accomplished. The Klisura Pass belonged to us. Late in the afternoon we reached the valley. Reconnaissance in the direction of Kastoria was underway. Height 800 arose in the background. The mountain dominated the approach to Kastoria and covered the III. Corps' withdrawal route. The attack on the height began at the first light of dawn. Again the shells howl away above us and bore into the masses of stone. But the Greek artillery is stronger. The heavy artillery fire teaches me that no overwhelming tactics can succeed here, and only a planned attack can succeed, Around noon the attack was repeated with the support of heavy artillery and the III. Battalion of the LAH."

On April 12, 1941 a British aerial bomb fell on the kitchen truck of the staff battery of the I. Unit. The departing motorcycle messenger Fritz Sieber was killed. He was the first to fall in the new Artillery Regiment. Obersturmführer Fritz Teufel (Chief, 1st Battery) was the first to reach the scene and gather the visibly stunned men.

Deeply moved, Teufel spoke the last words at the burial: "Comrade Sieber—You are the first—We greet you!"

Artillery Battle at Kastor Lake

The fifteenth of April 19412 entered the history of the still-young Artillery Regiment. As of 8:00 A.M. all the batteries moved into their firing positions. The enemy had well-constructed positions anmd favored all the units, especially the LAH Artillery, with the heaviest, well-observed fire. After just an hour's firefight the 2nd Battery was moved forward to fight down enemy positions with direct fire. The advance routes were under pinpoint fire, preventing all movement. About 1:00 P.M. all the targets fired on were accounted for, and around 1:30 the entire Artillery Regiment, under Standartenführer Staudinger, opened fire on Height 800 southwest of Kastoria Lake. Cannoneer 3, Karl-Friedrich Meyer, reported on the action of the heavy howitzer batteries:

"We took up position on a field of clover and unloaded large amounts of ammunition. At that moment the Greek artillery began to cover the flat valley before us with harrassing fire—and heavy-caliber fire at that. For safety's sake we began to dig holes for cover, in which the men could lie to avoid splinters. Then we received the order to fire and began targeting. After we had fired several rounds, we had to throw ourselves head over heels into the dirt. The enemy zeroed in on our firing position and took our breath away. The shells exploded loudly between our holes. Biting powder smoke blew over them, and clumps of dirt fell on us. Curses!—we had never known such war as this!

"Meanwhile the 4th Battery had gone into position a few hundred meters to our left and began to fire immediately. Now the enemy fire moved from us over to our sister battalion. We continued our fire at long range. But scarcely had our comrades of the next battery been forced to take cover when the Greeks again fired a series of heavy shells into our clover field.

"Then two 10.5-cm light howitzer batteries of the I. Unit went into position 200 meters to our right. With unbelievably heavy fire the light batteries opened up. But unfortunately, they too could not hit the enemy batteries. We of the heavy batteries could catch our breath, for the Greek batteries now fired with all their might on the 'ten-fives'. Anyone who has not experienced that can scarcely imagine what was going on in the long valley of Kastoria. All around us, very loud echoes bounced off the high mountain ranges. Firing and explosing constantly overlapped. There the fury of war was raging, a genuine artillery battle was going on. What the reconnaissance unit ahead of us was doing, we did not know. We had the impression that we four batteries formed the front line, for during the firefight the infantry moved forward through our positions to form a row of riflemen. The morning went on at length with the exchange of our own fire and the enemy's fire at us. In the process, we moved into a narrow, deep drainage ditch to take cover. We were all filled with anger because we could not attack the enemy artillery.

"That would have been quite possible for us; we could even see their muzzle flash. But the Commander was attacking Height 800 and directed the fire himself. The Greek artillery did not interest him. We learned that from the VB.

"The Battery Chief repeatedly requested permission by radio to take the enemy guns under fire or change positions to the rear to get out of their direct view.

"Around noon Heberer blew his top after the 2nd gun was knocked out by a direct hit and Comrades Schenderlein and Ulc were killed by shell fragments. Again connections to the Commander were made. The Battery Chief shouted into the microphone that he could no longer take responsibility for it, as his boys were being shot down! He reported that he was changing position immediately and soon would be ready to fire with three guns. In record time we moved the heavy howitzers out. The Greeks could not switch that fast, so we got away. We took up a safe position behind a hill on the western edge of the valley and immediately got back into the fight." How the fight went for the light batteries was told by Gunner Hartmann of the 2nd Battery: ""About 1:00 P.M. the 1st and 4th guns opened fire on Height 800. But the Greek artillery observer could see our position easily, so that the first enemy shells soon fell in the vicinity. We did not let them bother us at first. We could not dig ourselves in, as the ground was swampy. We soon suffered the first hit on our gun and the first wounded men. Then the battery officer commanded: "Everybody take full cover!" We had no holes to take cover in. Everybody made use of every little dip in the ground to find a little protection. Immediately the question came by phone from the command post as to why we were no longer firing. Ust. Lohse answered:

Above: *The armed reconnaissance unit advances over the Klisura Pass (1385 meters) toward Kastoria Lake. The road over the pass is so narrow that the tractors and the heavy guns scarcely have enough room (see title description).* Below: *Two radiomen of the 1st Battery are under Greek artillery fire. Slowly they crawl toward a command post with their heavy radios.*

"We have heavy enemy artillery fire on our position!" The battery officer replied: "The infantry urgently needs our artillery support!" At that the aiming gunner of our first gun jumped up, loaded, aimed and fired—breech open, cartridge case thrown out, new shell into the barrel, cartridge after it, breech closed, aim, fire.

"While dirt and fragments flew around his ears, he cared only about his gun. He could still hear the words: 'The Infantry urgently needs our help!' After several shots, the K2 also jumped up and took part in this merciless firefight. Now the 4th gun was also firing. The ripping explosions and the noise of firing mixed with each other. The cannoneers worked feverishly. The two gunners fired 72 shells from the first gun alone, until the infantry had reached Height 800 and the order came to cease fire."

"In this hour, on April 15, 1941, an unforgettable day for the whole battery, Unterscharführer Wenhart was killed by a shell fragment. Cannoneers Felke, Gotzmann, Heine, Heldt, Lindenthal and Medecke were wounded. Unterscharführer Krause, the medic, was hit in the left hip by shell fragments while he was bandaging the wounded.

"When it was quiet, the Regimental Commander called the firing position and asked who the cannoneers were who had kept the guns firing. He had been able to observe the moving scene from his position and stated at once that the men would be recommended for the Iron Cross II. A few days later the men stood before their Commander, Sepp Dietrich, and received the bravely earned decorations from his hand."

Under cover of the artillery fire, the infantry units had worked their way to the foot of the hill. The enemy fire continued until about 3:30 P.M., when a dive-bomber attack silenced the batteries forever.

"Unload on the Green artillery, unload!" the cannoneers shouted eagerly to the skies. And in fact the flying comrades had come to help. "They're shooting up my artillery regiment!" Sepp Dietrich shouted from his command post, requesting quick air support. Sepp Dietrich also respected the actions of Battery Chief Heberer, who had saved human lives and materials from destruction by a clever position change against orders. The fruits of victory could be gained by the reconnaissance unit, which hurried toward Kastoria en masse in the evening, captured numerous surprised enemy columns with 12,000 men, and took 36 guns.

Untersturmführer Hans Bernhard as observation officer of the heavy battery (5./SS-AR "LSSAH"). Notable landmarks and spotted enemy positions were noted precisely on the map. The folding card table proved to be very practical.

The fight against the crowded Greek Army went on. Under considerable difficulties, the LSSAH overwhelmed the Metsoven Pass and compelled 16 divisions of the Epirus and Macedonian Army to surrender. The surrender was signed by Sepp Dietrich and General Tzolakoglou at Larissa on April 21, 1941. Practically on its own, the Leibstandarte had decided the campaign by its fast advance. This led to all kinds of diplomatic friction, since the Greeks had surrendered to the LAH but were not regarded as conquered by the Italians, who wanted to set terms. But the Supreme Commander, deeply moved by the victory of the Leibstandarte, had to make political arrangements. Thus talks took place between Dietrich and the Italian General Rossi.

The men of the LSSAH had a very friendly relationship with the Greek soldiers. The prisoners sat on the gun carriages and rode homeward with their conquerors.

- What pictures!

Above: *The firing position of the 2nd Battery near Kastoria Lake. Ceaseless fire is aimed at the Greeks and is answered with unbelievable intensity.* Below: *Fritz Will and Walter Staudinger are seen husbanding their strength during a short pause in the battle. Witt fell on the invasion front on June 14, 1944 as Commander of the 12th SS Armored Division "Hitler Youth."*

Above: *The First Battery crosses the Aliakmon near Grevena on April 18, 1941. The march led over the crater-riddled road with its steep grades and curves.* Below: *The rocky mountain roads made extreme demands on the trucks and tractors. The repair services had to work extra hard. They worked on the vehicles feverishly to finish changing the pads on the tracks. Damage in the rocky terrain was enormous.*

Above: *The Greek surrender has taken place. Relaxation and rest for Max Wünsche and Walter Staudinger. The Commander remains serious—the battle is not over yet! They have to take up the pursuit of the British troops.* Below: *The stormiest part of the sdvance begins. Its goal is the Gulf of Patras! Through Agrinon and Mesolongion to the fishing village of Navpaktos, directly on the Gulf, reached in the evening hours of April 26, 1941 by the strengthened Reconnaissance Unit (with the 2nd Battery).*

Above: *At high speed the head of the 1st Battery follows, with Oberscharführer Wilhelm Auge in the jeep.* Below: *The observation post and firing position of the 1st Battery are located at the old lighthouse in Navpaktos, right on the shore of the Gulf. Unterscharführer Hans Stoff (+) operates the shear scope as SFU, while Sturmmann Kretschmer takes a look at the Peloponnes.*

Obergruppenführer Sepp Dietrich supervises the embarcation of his troops in Navpaktos. The LAH fleet consisted chiefly of captured fishing boats.

In the morning hours of April 27, 1941 the 1st Battery fires into the Gulf to keep sighted boats away from the Navpaktos-Patras transport line. The gunner taking the pictures was so excited by the firing that he twisted the picture.

In a fast advance, the strengthened Reconnaissance Unit of the Leibstandarte, with the 2nd Battery, reached the coast at the entrance to the Gulf of Corinth.

The Commander of the Reconnaissance Unit, Sturmbannführer Meyer (Panzermeyer), stood on the pier at Navpaktos, a small medieval harbor with defensive turrets, on April 26, 1941. He decided to cross the Gulf with his unit at once and take the harbor town of Patras. The surprise attack succeeded. On account of the great distance, the landing place could not be taken under fire by the artillery. The batteries, though, took up firing positions directly on the shore to protect the coast. The 1st Battery was at the old lighthouse in Navpaktos and covered the lively ferry traffic. The undertaking was a success.

On the Peloponnes contact could be made with the paratroopers. This completed the combat actions.

The Leibstandarte, as a fast motorized unit, stood out not only on the cart tracks in the mountains but also in maritime experiences.

After the battles ended, the units took up resting positions near Larissa.

At the troop training camp of Wischau in the Protectorate of Bohemia and Moravia, the Leibstandarte was reinforced. The Artillery Regiment received a second 8.8 cm Flak battery.

A Heavy Field Howitzer 18 (sFH 18), 149 mm caliber, with a range of 13,325 meters and a rate of four shots per minute, weighed 5,542 kilograms in firing position.

Victory Parade in Athens Before Field Marshal List

Above: *Before the royal palace in Athens, the Field Marshal (left) views the parade on May 3, 1941. On the podium of honor, SS Obergruppenführer Sepp Dietrich, Commander of the Leibstandarte, stands at the right.* Below: *A battery or company of every unit of the LSSAH takes part. Behind the 3rd Battery (Horns), which served with the light artillery unit, are the heavy howitzers of the 4th Battery under Hauptsturmführer Fritz Schröder.*

Light Field Howitzer 18 (le. FH 18)
Caliber: 105 mm
Range: 10,675 meters
Rate of fire: 6-8 rounds per minute
Weight in firing position: 1985 kilograms

The leader of the motorcycle courier squad of the 1st Unit, Uscha. Schulz-Raase, was lost on the "Road of Death" on the way back to Slawisch Brod when he was struck by a towbar that broke loose. The photo shows him a few days before at the staff battery's motor pool. As a heavy weapons man he wears the General Assault Medal, and days later he received the Iron Cross II.

2

First Russian Action 1941-42

On June 20, 1941 the Leibstandarte received orders to march out of their billet area at Brünn/Wischau. Among the soldiers there was much puzzling over their possible action. The news of an attack on the Soviet Union struck like a bolt of lightning. On the evening of June 22, 1941 the transport trains with the men of the LSSAH headed for Germany's eastern boundary. On June 30, 1941 the troops crossed the Russian border near Uscilug. They were assigned to be the reserves of the Armored Group I/Army Group South (Field Marshal von Rundstedt). Kiev was to be moved on quickly. The Russian forces west of the Dniepr were to be shattered in the process.

The advance took place on the Armored Road "North", better known under the name of "Rollbahn Nord". The III. Army Corps was enclosed near Rovno and was to be liberated by a surprise attack of the Leibstandarte.

On July 2, 1941 the guns of the Artillery Regiment first moved into an assigned firing position. On the very next day the I. Unit encountered attacking Soviet tanks near Klevan. They were fired on immediately by the observant 1st Battery of Obersturmführer Teufel. Rottenführer Franz Müntzel stood out as the aiming gunner of a light howitzer used in direct fire. He succeeded in shooting down the first tank for the Artillery Regiment with high-angle fire. Previously, only the 8.8 cm Flak gun had been successful as a "tank destroyer". The joy over this success was great. Before the Artillery Regiment was established in 1940, the then IV. Unit of AR-VT had also shot down French tanks with direct lFH 18 fire in the French campaign (at, among other places, La Fouillouse/St. Etienne).

Again and again there was heavy fighting with overwhelmed and scattered Red Army men who were trying to rejoin their troops. Here in Russia the terrain was undependable everywhere. The greatest caution, including that of supply troops, was required, especially at night. Hastening columns were attacked and motor vehicles struck by mines. The war in the east set new and different standards than had been known previously. During the LSSAH's long advance on the Rollbahn Nord in the direction of Shitomir, the light artillery column of the I. Unit had to carry on bitter combat.

A radioman of the 2nd Battery recalled: The intelligence squad of our battery was in an areas with poor visibility. The road was 200 meters away from us. On the other side of the road was a forest, from the cover of which the Red Armny constantly threatened our flanks. Here I saw how several prisoners claimed to be Ukrainian. These soldiers came to us full of hope. Unfortunately, in battle we had no time to deal with them suitably. We sent most of them to the backlines without escort.

Our artillery column, which was behind us to one side, had to withstand a wild attack. After they had taken prisoners by surprise, they had to fight off two other enemy groups. Becoming cautious, they secured all around the camp and formed a hedgehog defense. Russian units made attacks on it. It took several hours until all the attacks were beaten off. Here Untersturmführer Taut, weaponmaster of the Artillery Regiment, stood out in close combat. He was able to wipe out several machine-gun nests in personal combat, for which he received the Iron Cross I. The fighting showed that even supply units were threatened in combat against the Soviets. There was no safety anywhere. The enemy was everywhere, thus danger was everywhere. We had to be very watchful."

On July 12, 1941 vthe 6th Battery was pushed in, with their four heavy Flak guns, between the Reconnaissance Unit and the 1st Battalion. A Soviet attack of at least battalion strength came to a stop under heavy Flak fire just short of the road. The battery dug itself in and shot down further attacks. Some Russians cut through as far as the limbers' position. They were wiped out at dawn by the surveying squad and the limber crews under the command of Staff Squad Leader Theidigsmann. The Troop Doctor, Dr. von Paternos, who had set up his dressing station there, mopped up the area in close combat.

The excellent shooting of the Soviet artillery, which had only selected and very intelligent men in its ranks, was especially noticeable. It required hard work to knock out the enemy batteries. Sometimes enemy artillery observers, who often took positions on windmills and silos, had to be taken out by direct fire of the light howitzer batteries. In Dolczyk, Obersturmführer Saul of the 2nd

Loading the Staff Battery (1st Unit) for the eastern front. Typical railroad cars were the two-axle flatcars of the "Stuttgart" type.

The sad faces of Erich Meyer and Hermann Juhls of the 1st Battery show no jubilation or enthusiasm.

Above: *"Fire!" The K II grabs the firing lanyard and fires. After the barrel advances, he opens the breech and takes out the cartridge case. The K 1 aiming gunner immediately takes aim. The gun is operated by a gun leader and five gunners. Usually, though, there were fewer.* Below: *Ammunition supplies for the 1st Battery. Shell baskets and cases lie ready to be taken. The ammunition squads with their heavy and medium trucks were responsible for that. The ammo squad leader (in a medium personnel vehicle) guarded the supplies.*

July 12, 1941, Rollbahn Nord: Captured Red Army men are questioned
While columns move westward to prison camp, Unit Commander Sukkau, born in Berdjansk, talks with a 15-year-old soldier. He was sent home to his parents.

Captured Russian heavy "Maxim" machine guns at Sokolov-Gestell on the Rollbahn Nord, July 11-12, 1941. The light artillery column under the command of Weaponmaster Taut captured a large quantity of war materials and took many prisoners.

Battery utilized excellent fire control. He was badly wounded several days later. As early as July 14, 1941 it was noted in the daily report of the LSSAH that artillery ammunition was urgently needed.

After only two weeks of action there was already a shortage of ammunition! At Zhurchnaya the 2nd Battery was thus not able to fire on a railroad line known to be used by military trains. Only the 1st and 3rd Batteries fired 40 AZ (impact-fuze shells) apiece at the nearby village.

On July 22, 1941 the batteries were removed from their firing positions and sent to a new place of action southeast of Shitomir, the target being Sokolovka. A connection was made with the 16th Armored Division, and the Teolin area was reached. For the LSSAH attack on July 30, 1941 the I. Unit was assigned to the I. Battalion.

At 7:00 A.M. Zibermanovka had already been taken, and the infantry companies were digging themselves in at the edge of the village of Yarovtka. A recognized enemy battery was knocked out by the 2./AR-LSSAH.

At 10:45 a Russian tank attack moved through Yarovtka and rolled ponderously forward. It was driven back by direct fire from the lFH 18 guns of the 1st Battery, with help from the tank destroyers. The 1st Battery could paint more rings on their barrels, but the advance observer, Untersturmführer Wilhelm Afflerbach, was lost.

Heavy Russian artillery fire fell on Yarovtka. All the batteries worked hard to repulse the enemy. During the battle, the Fend Battery (8.8 cm Flak) fired on the railroad station in Zibermanovka, which was still in Soviet hands. Their fire with armor-piercing and explosive shells caused flames to rise high into the sky. After the town was taken, it was found that two ammunition trains had been hit and were completely burned out. Only the iron ribs of the cars still stood on the tracks. Another tank attack was driven back after 4:00 P.M. The sector was held against the heaviest enemy pressure. Toward evening, after the Russians had ceased their activities, The batteries prepared barrage fire for the combat sector of the 1st Battalion and the reconnaissance unit. When the fighting ended, the Leibstandarte SS Adolf Hitler was transferred farther south, to the Talnoye area, on July 31, 1941. It was to strengthen the ring surrounding the big pocket at Uman and prevent the Soviet Army from breaking out to the north near Novo Archangelsk. In this area there was a gap through which the Russians wanted to break. In the evening hours of August 1, 1941 there was already a strong tank attack from the woods east of Novo Archangelsk, but it came to a stop under the fire of the I. Unit. One tank sustained a direct hit from an lFH 18. In the next few days constantly repeated desperation attacks of the Red Army were fought off. The main Soviet forces were turning away from the pressure of the German divisions coming from the west and against that of the LSSAH, which was able, despite heavy losses, to hold the position in spite of great pressure from the enemy. Near Novo-Archangelsk the troops experienced for the first time a massive gathering of artillery. An Army 21 cm mortar battery and a foglaying instructional regiment were subordinated to the LSSAH. The wooded areas were taken under fire by the foglayers. This first use of the new weapon impressed the artillerymen greatly and caused the enemy much confusion. Even the men of the LSSAH were unnerved at first by the howling and screeching rockets. The ring around the pocket was pulled tighter and tighter, and all counterattacks were shot down in the concerted fire of the heavy weapons. On August 5, 1941 all available weapons were turned on the enemy in the woods northwest of Novo-Archangelsk. The fire of the LAH artillery and the subordinated Army batteries was concentrated on the wooded areas. It was as if hell had opened its throat. For the first firing the 2nd Battery was assigned 200 rounds. Panzermeyer wrote in his book *Grenadiere*: "Over us there was a sickening howl. Thick plumes of smoke floated away above us and disappeared between the trees. Without a pause, fiery rockets hissed toward the enemy. The heavy shells of the mortars rolled through the air like freight trains and completed the noise of the Do-launchers. The woods burst apart like an anthill under the foot of a giant beast. The destruction sickened me." Three days later the great encircling battle came to an end. The LSSAH was at the focal point of the battle and had prevented all furious attempts to break out.

During the further advance, the 2nd Battery rolled eastward under the command of Hauptsturmführer Adolf Cischek, along with the Reconnaissance Unit. The battery became Panzermeyer's "house battery". Horst Mutterlose, then a communications man, reported: "We had to get used to the Sturmbannführer's unorthodox way of fighting. On the evening of August 10, as we arrived, we were sent into infantry action with the motorcycle couriers. Here and only much later it occurred to me that the commander of the Reconnaissance Unit counted on every man. There were no supply men where he was. Every shoemaker, tailor or cook was sent into battle when needed. Our 2nd Battery always went into position quickly to fire explosive shells at retreating Soviets, and the effect of the shells was fearful. After that we were told to be ready to march out at once and join the column of the AA."

Above: *The motorcycle courier of a light battery is at the head of the attack. Assault guns, still fitted with short guns ("stubs"), open the way.* Below: *A heavy howitzer fires steadily to the east from the dusty road.*

Sturmbannführer Alexander Sukkau discusses the situation with the commander of the 1st Battalion, Knight's Cross bearer Fritz Witt, to whom the I. Unit was subordinated, to knock out large enemy groups.

Ludwig Kalischko as SS Untersturmführer and Battery Officer of the 1st Battery. From 1944 on, as an SS Hauptsturmführer, Kalischko led the 1st (armored) Unit and went missing in the retreat combat near Varpalota, Hungary.

The farther the Leibstandarte moved eastward, the greater their losses were. Graves along the Rollbahn Nord included that of Norbert Ziembka, 3rd Battery.

A BMW radio car advances through blistering heat with the Juhls/Meyer radio troop (1st Battery).

Oberscharführer Auge (far left) with his intelligence squad. Helmut Klockmann holds the radio antenna upright. Radiomen Meier (+), Juhls and Meyer work on the Type B radios.

The 1st Battery supported the advance of the 1st Company. Radioman Knapp (with steel helmet) and his radio served under the Company Chief, SS Hauptsturmführer Gerd Pleiss (+), who held the Knight's Cross.

After the pocket of Uman was closed, Hermann Juhls (+), Kurt Brinkmann (+), Anton Zettlemeissl (+) and Erich Meyer (left to right) are seen in the woods near Novo-Archangelsk.

The Fight for Sasselye

The advance of the strengthened Reconnaissance Unit went further to the south toward Sasselye on August 13, 1941. The town was reached around 7:15 P.M. Here it was surrounded by newly arrived enemy forces.

Without connections to the Standarte, strengthened only by the 2nd Battery, the Reconnaissance Unit fought against strong enemy groups.

The 2nd Battery had an observation post in the church steeple and thus had an ideal panoramoc view. From there, every preparation for action could be seen early. Normally, artillery observation points were supposed to avoid prominent points in the terrain, but here they didn't go by the book. Here it was "Sight is more important than cover!" The radiomen had set up their Berta and Dora sets some time ago.

On the afternoon of August 14, 1941 Sasselye was attacked, once from the east, then from the south.

As the events unfolded, the enemy suffered heavy losses from the superb defensive fire of the 2nd Battery. But the Russian artillery also joined in and caused disturbances. The town was under steady Russian artillery fire. Under this cover, the Russians worked their way close to town in the fields of corn, some of which was high.

Every hour reinforcements from the 1st Battery were counted on. The ammunition and fuel supplies were supposed to be sent through. But the advance was disturbed by heavy air attacks on the column. Only shortly before dark did Obersturmführer Heinrich Springer with the reinforced 3rd Company arrive as the first unit of the I. Battalion, which was coming to provide reinforcement. The 1st Battery under Fritz Teufel was also near, taking a position north of Sasselye and firing eastward. The observation officer of the 1st Battery, Untersturmführer Horst Hermann Lau, was lost there.

In the evening Sturmbannführer Kurt Meyer set up the town for all-around defense. All available men had to serve as sentries in the foxholes. Panzermeyer himself checked the security measures, A radioman reported:

"He asked us: 'Well, boys, are we holding everything?'—'Of course! Just let them come. We'll handle them easily!' Our answers showed our youthful confidence, trust in our weapons and our leader. We were firmly convinced of our striking power. Those were not just empty words. Panzermeyer instinctively did the right thing there. He sought to learn the mood of his trusted men. By our appearance he knew exactly what he could depend on us for. Every man received cigarettes from him.

"Around 8:00 P.M. he ordered all the heavy weapons to stop firing for the night. On the morning of the next day, all artilerymen, to the last man, were on infantry duty. Only the cooks could still cook the food and be the silent reserves."

A further attack on Sasselye was reported. Horst Mutterlose recalls: "When the Red Army moved toward the village, an Obersturmführer called: 'Let them come to 50 meters. Open fire only at my command!' Hesitant at first, but coming at us standing, then creeping and crawling, they thought they'd surprise us. All at once we opened fire. The unbearable tension in us was released. We noticed every movement, shot from all buttonholes. The Russians were completely surprised. They lay on the ground as if mown down. Our scout cars pushed far forward, rounded up the enemies and drove the survivors to our positions at the edge of town. We took many prisoners."

In all, 651 men were captured, and more than 200 lay dead on the ground. The Russian Rifle Regiment 962 was wiped out. The regimental commander and most of the officers had shot themselves already (so the prisoners said).

The fight for Sasselye went on. Russian Flak fired on the church steeple; five of the intelligence men were wounded. But the steeple was not deserted. This good observation post allowed a complete view of the battlefield. Constantly the artillerymen informed Panzermeyer, whose command post was in a bus in the vicinity. Since the Russians never attacked concentrically, the motorcycle riflemen could be directed effectively to the threatened areas.

In the early morning hours of August 16, 1941 another attack on Sasselye took place from the southwest. It was completely shattered by artillery fire. Five kilometers to the west, strong enemy columns were spotted moving southward. All our forces were needed to defend against the enemies, who were attacking from all sides.

With mobile defense by constantly moving armored scout cars, the fronts on the edge of town were held. A heavy Russian battery took a position that was immediately fired on by the 2nd Battery.Only after some time could it be smashed with help from the heavy battery. Men of Army Infantry Regiment 60 fought their way to Sasselye. They admired the men of the Leibstandarte for fighting off all the attacks so calmly.

"Panzermeyer" set up the town for all-around defense. His machine pistol is close at hand, for the situation is dangerous. Young Ukrainians describe the terrain.

Armored scout cars of the Reconnaissance Unit were used decisively in the fighting around Sasselye. This photo came from the Greek campaign.

Around 11:40 A.M. the Russians tried again, with reinforcements, to break through from the east. They were fanatical attackers from the Odessa NCO School. Meanwhile the link with Army IR 60 was lost, but it could be restored late in the afternoon. Around 6:00 P.M. another bomb attack was made on Sasselye. Only then did the enemy see that it was impossible to win the fight against the bitterly defending Leibstandarte. The way to the south was open. Kherson was already under durect attack on August 19, 1941.

The Taking of Kherson

The attack on Kherson was led along the Dniepr to the harbor road by, among others, the reinforced Reconnaissance Unit. By 12:50 P.M. it had taken the Dniepr shore east of Kherson. The Russians crossed to the opposite shore with all kinds of water craft, from freight boats to rowboats. Panzermeyer wanted to stop the crossing. The 2nd Battery was to fire on the boats. Since no time was to be lost, the howitzers were fired directly. The 1st Platoon under Oberscharführer Meyer moved forward to the front line. The historian of the 2nd Battery told of the ensuing firefight:

"Two light howitzers of our battery were moved up to the Dniepr crossing. The ferries and gunboats were attacked with direct fire. Panzermeyer stood next to the guns and personally indicated the targets. With 52 shots a towboat was sunk and a gunboat damaged so that it turned back. After the very first shots the Russian crossing suddenly stopped. The enemy was really confused! Sturmbannführer Meyer rejoiced withus artillerymen as we hit the targets with our shells. Now it was clear what remarkable luck this Panzermeyer had. While the light howitzers continued firing on recognized, worthwhile targets, he left the firing position. Scarcely was he gone than the platoon was fired on by Russian 12.2 cm cannon howitzers that stood on the slope on the other side of the Dniepr. The guns were in effect offered on a platter. The rain of fragments fell on the gunners. In no time we had one dead (Kaiser) and four wounded. The others were able to save themselves at the last minute by jumping into a limestone ditch. The guns had to be pulled to cover by manpower. Gerhard Schmidt died on the way to the dressing station."

After most of the Leibstandarte had pushed into Kherson, there was another "sea battle" at the harbor. Heavy weapons of all kinds took part. Dr. Naumann's Flak battery was able to sink two gunboats that wanted to escape to the Black Sea.

Radio troops with their canister sets advance on Sasselye.

Russian artillery shells land on the German limber park.

Burned-out supply vehicles of the 2nd Battery in Sasselye.

After the battle ended, the 2nd Battery's dead were buried.

Graves were dug by the church in Sasselye.

Horst Kirchhof and Georg Klimke have found their last resting place.

Every intelligence squad had not only two telephone troops but also several (at least three) radio troops, which maintained the connections between the individual parts of the battery. Walter Nofts of the 2nd Battery has received a message.

An Adler telephone truck of the Intelligence Squad (1st Battery) resting at the mouth of the Dniepr. Oberscharführer Augeuses his suitcase radio to cheer up Hans Metz (chief's driver) and Stoffers (SDG).

The Commander of the Leibstandarte awards the Iron Cross 1st and 2nd Classes to officers of the Artillery Regiment near Bobrinez. His adjutant Max Wünsche (2rd from left) was later Commander of the SS Armored Regiment "HJ"(Hitler-Jugend).

The Leibstandarte SS Adolf Hitler advanced to the isthmus of Crimea in mid-September 1941. The terrain is flat here and almost without cover. How the fast advances into enemy country worked out for the men who followed a short way behind was described by Sturmmann Mutterlose of the 2nd Battery: "A vehicle breakdown left us stranded beside the road. The radiator water had trickled into the dust. We needed water to make repairs and thus went off to a village to the side of the main road. To get to the well, we thus had to leave our advance route. The well was amid a group of houses. The sun was hot and we six men, like the crew of our repair truck, sweated heavily. Gradually the villagers came out. They were friendly though hesitant. We were the first German soldiers they had been able to see close-up. Although we worked all day without a break, it got dark before we were finished with the job. Now, since the night was coming on, driving farther was unthinkable. So we had to stay in the village overnight. The 17th of September began with a wonderful sunrise. It was about 5:00 A.M. when we loaded our weapons into the trucks and got ready to march away. We just wanted to eat breakfast, for who knew when we would have time again? We sat on several canisters with our backs to a haystack. I had just taken a hearty drink from my field flask when a Russian officer jumped out from behind the haystack with a loud yell. His left hand held a rifle; in his right hand he had a grenade ready to throw. The distance between me and the Ivan was about ten meters. There was no time to think. Instinctively, I got up and was about to jump on the officer. But he had acted faster and thrown his hand grenade. The detonation pressure threw me far forward. Shots were heard from all over. More hand grenades flew, and I heard cries and shouts as well. 'Play dead!', that was the only thing that occurred to me in this situation. It was clear to me that we were surrounded.

"There I lay with blood trickling out of my mouth. Although I lay monionless, I felt a hard blow on my right shin. So I was still a target. Then the attack suddenly ended. Carefully I raised my head to observe the scene. I shouldn't have done that, because several Russians were looking right at me. My wallet stuck sideways out of my back pocket, for my jacket had been pulled up. They immediately pulled it out and looked through it. . Besides my paybook and photos, I had collected Russian exemption permits, which airplanes had often dropped along the road. Since they were badly made, they inspired our satire and thus attracted my interest. As if at a command they grabbed me, two men with my hands and feet, and off they went with me at a run."

Obergruppenführer Dietrich meets with the Artillery Regiment before they reached Crimea and explains the situation to the leaders gathered around Standartenführer Staudinger.

On the Plains of the Nogaish Steppe

Above: *The 2nd Battery has taken a new firing position. After the tractors leave the position, the ammunition squad comes in and unloads quickly. To avoid a cluster of vehicles it is practical to unload the ammo trucks near the guns.* Below: *Fire!—The barrel recoils. Shell after shell hums away toward the enemy.*

The initial gunfire is used to home in, and in some cases (such as pinpoint fire) also to fire on targets. Group fire and salvoes have their effect, particularly to utilize important moments in the battle.

Karl Gross and Horst Jakob (+) at the Anton gun of the 2nd Battery in a firefight. The gun bears the name "Riki," the name of a gunner's girlfriend.

Untershcarführer Erich Dinter, A Gun Leader, was wounded several times at his gun. Karl Gross checks the settings on the panoramic scope.

A pause in the fight! Dinter's gun crew enjoys a hearty casserole. Shortly thereafter, Obergruppenführer Dietrich appeared at the gun and ate with his artillerymen as they sat on the spars of the lFH 18. The respected commander shared container and spoon with gunner Kurt Fentrup.

"I groaned loudly as they carried me, less from pain than from desperation. I tried to see the faces of the Red Army men. They were young, inexperienced soldiers. Then suddenly there was a detonation! In the direction of our truck I saw a plume of smoke rising. Remarkably, at that moment the four of them simply let me fall. All I saw was the backsides of the dirt-brown Russians and their leggings trotting across the steppe. Now my will to live awakened and I struggled back with all my energy. When I reached a stable, I stood up and limped onward as best I could. The first thing I saw was our good truck in flames, burning brightly. Then I saw my always-quiet comrade Heinz lying there, right where we had eaten ten minutes ago. I grabbed Heinz by the shoulder, shook him and yelled in desperation: 'Heinz, let's get going!' But Heinz couldn't answer me. He was silenced forever. Again I looked around, but I saw no trace of my missing comrades. Now I limped toward the burning truck, tore the door open, grabbed my belt with the bullet pouches, threw everything over my blood-smeared head and took the rifle out of its holster. I stumbled back to the road and met a group of our 1st Battalion (Witt). Finally I was safe.

Only very much later did I learn that my four missing comrades safely reached the unit. Unarmed when attacked, they had done the only right thing: made a fast exit by zigzagging across the steppe."

The survey battery of the Artillery Regiment finally cleaned out the village and took numerous prisoners. The Battery Chief, Hauptsturmführer Müller, then occupied a kolkhoze in a surprise attack. This success gave Müller impetus. The survey battery of the LSSAH then attacked field positions expanded by the infantry. But the Russians recornized that they were being attacked by only a small unit and fought off the attack. A member of the battery reported:

"About two kilometers outside Gromovka in the neighborhood of the isthmus near Genitchesk we were fired on from a hay shed, and we attacked immediately. Heavy rifle fire and grenade bursts cut into our ranks. We were able to capture several Russians. In front of me was an officer with a pistol. When I brought him in, he jumped into a foxhole, and I jumped in right behind him. He tried to reach his pistol, but I was faster. I immediately took it away from him, through his cap across the area and showed him the way to the west. Meanwhile my comrades had gone farther, and I followed them. To the right I saw Schäfer the 'Spiess' with his peaked cap and drawn pistol, attacking in the opposite direction.

"Scarcely had I covered 300 meters when I lay in the dust of the steppe. The Russian fire was so heavy that I couldn't move. We were stuck in front of a dug-out position. When things quieted down a bit, I crawled back.

"In this action the Soviets had cleverly lured us into a trap. As a result we lost ten dead and just as many wounded.

"Late in the afternoon a search troop of volunteers was assembled. All the dead and wounded had already been taken by the Russians. We didn't find anybody."

Breakthrough to Crimea

On September 23, 1941 the Artillery Regiment of the LSSAH was on the march to the 73rd Infantry Division, to which it was subordinated for the breakthrough on the isthmus.

The whole artillery action was turned over to Arko 20. Along with the LAH artillery, two other Army units were available. The 1st Unit (Sukkau) was subordinated to the infantry battle group, Arko 110.

During the next day the infantry divisions (73 and 46), supported by the engineers and the strong and well-directed artillery, were able to break five kilometers into the fortified position at Perekop.

The battle report of the 2nd Battery/AR0LSSAH states for September 24, 1941:

"From 4:00 to 4:30 the 1st Unit, along with several Army units, and after another check of the firing situation, made attacks of artillery fire on Preobrashenka.

"At 4:45 the order came to fire on Point 627; it was carried out at 5:10.

"At 9:00 the battery moved its position to a hedge 500 meters east of Settlement AP 15. From there the battery made two attacks (planned firing on targets given by the unit).

"The advanced observers of the 1st and 2nd Batteries were with the II./Infantry Regiment 186, the Battery Chief of the 2nd Battery with the III./IR 187, to support the advance of the battalion from there.

"At 11:30 the order came to fire on Brigitte, which was knocked out with 42 shots at 11:40.

"At 5:30 P.M. the battery changed its position again, to 600 meters northwest of Preobrashenka.

Fire control for the 3rd Battery by the advanced observer (Rothe). Through the shear scope the strikes are observed and the aim corrected. The radioman passes the values on to the battery officer in the firing position.

The unit ordered the battery leaders to [p. 64] the commander of I./IR 186, which was to attack the Tatar moat northwest of the railway at dawn tomorrow, in order to take action there. While looking for the battalion's command post, Sturmmann Ohst was badly wounded. Unterscharführer Friedrich and Sturmmann Kirschner died a heroic death."

The newly-formed cannon battery also received its baptism of fire.

It saw action along with the II. Unit and added a valuable dimension to the Artillery Regiment.

On September 25, 1941 too, the Artillery Regiment and Engineer Battalion of the LSSAH saw action without change on the isthums with the breakthrough divisions.

The continuation of the 2nd Battery's combat report for September 25 says: "In the first hours of the morning, the unit's command post and the positions of the 1st and 2nd Batteries were laid out 500 meters south of Point 656. From there the battery fired on the enemy fortresses north of the railway at Point 659 to support the attack of the III./IR 170 and make the advance on both sides of the railway line possible.

"At 10:00 A.M. the battery again changed positions to 1.5 km south of Preobrashenka. From there the battery again fired on fortifications near Point 659. At 2:00 P.M. the 1st and 2ndBatteries received the order to cover the advance of the I./IR 186 on the Tatar ditch to the southeast.

"At 5:30 P.M. the batteries zeroed in on the Tatar wall, since the I./IR 186 was to attack the wall on September 26, 1941.

"At 4:00 P.M. the battery, along with several other batteries, directed concentrated fire at an enemy tank attack. In all, nine tanks were destroyed."

All the batteries' observation posts were constantly under enemy fire. A direct hit killed Fritz Grosse of the 3rd Battery. The VB of the 1st Battery, Untersturmführer Karl Vath, was badly wounded by an explosive shell. Thus the 1st Battery lost its third observation officer in a few weeks. Unterscharführer Sepp Aichholzer was gravely wounded by a direct hit. Both of the fallen men were remembered by the awarding of the Iron Cross I in August 1942. It was a nice gesture of the later battery chief De Vries, since Iron Crosses were always given to the batteries in certain numbers, At this time such decorations were still possible; later the decorations became fewer and fewer, very much against the general trend.

The 73rd Infantry Division took Perekop on September 26, 1941. The 46th Infantry Division found itself in a hard fight near Armyansk. The final report of the 2nd Battery: "26.9.41, from 5:30 to 5:50 A.M., effective fire on the Tatar ditch.

"At 5:40 the I./IR 186 attacked the ditch and took it without strong resistance. Dive bombers had achieved good effects with their almost pauseless attacks.

"At 11:00 A.M. the battery changed position to the rear and took up a new position 600 meters east of Point 663. The battery's observation post was on the Tatar wall. From there Arnyansk was fired on effectively with 100 observed rounds.

"At 4:30 P.M. our VB Ulrich fired on three enemy tanks with one gun and compelled them to turn away. The firing position was repeatedly attacked by enemy bombs and ratas. In the evening the battery received the order to prepare to march out, as it was again to be subordinated to the Reconnaissance Unit."

At 4:15 P.M. Infantry Regiment 72 of the 46th Infantry Division penetrated into Armyansk. The Leibstandarte's batteries were withdrawn late in the evening.

For their cooperation in opening the Crimean isthmus, the men of the Artillery Regiment were awarded the Crimea Shield. This decoration was given in the autumn of 1943 (see the decoration certificate). They were supposed to reach the Tatar Ditch.

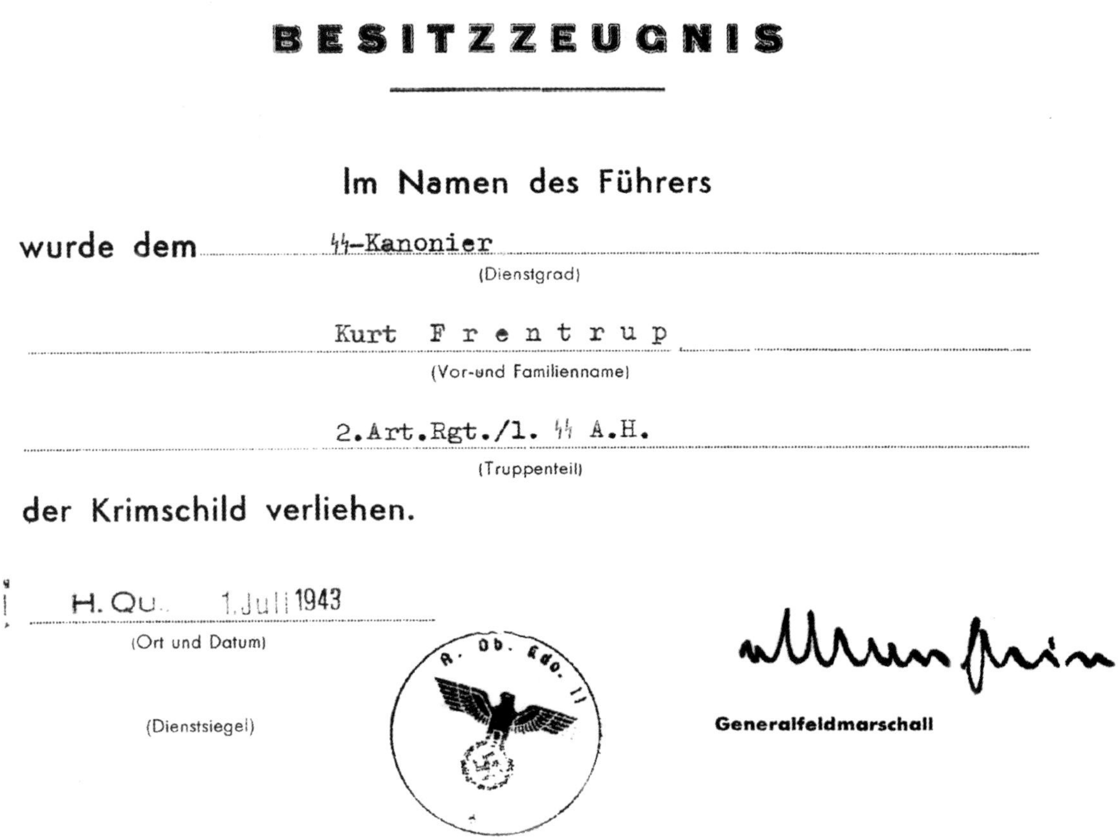

BESITZZEUGNIS

Im Namen des Führers

wurde dem SS-Kanonier
(Dienstgrad)

Kurt Frentrup
(Vor-und Familienname)

2.Art.Rgt./1. SS A.H.
(Truppenteil)

der Krimschild verliehen.

H. Qu. 1. Juli 1943
(Ort und Datum)

(Dienstsiegel)

Generalfeldmarschall

On July 25, 1942 Hitler awarded the Crimea Shield, to be worn on the left upper arm, for participation in the Crimean combat. The prerequisite was participation in one of the main battles. For the artillerymen of the Leibstandarte this was the breakthrough battle near Perekop (1st main battle).

Tatar Ditch, September 26, 1941—The VB of the 1st Battery, Unterscharführer Alois Plattner (+), checks the shot values with his battery chief Fritz Teufel. In front is Radioman Knapp with his carbine and Berta radio.

Sturmbannführer Dr. Schwab, Commander of the Glau Artillery School, makes observations at Perekop, along with Panzermeyer (with Knight's Cross) and Sturmbannführer Schönberger (Commander of Tracked Units, LSSAH, later of the Armored Troops), of the use of the newly integrated cannon battery. At left is the Battery Chief, Hst. Eric Urbanitz.

The 10 cm Cannon Battery joined the Leibstandarte on September 23, 1941 and experienced its baptism of fire on the Crimean isthmus just a few hours later.

Above: *After the Tatar Ditch was taken on September 26, 1941.* Below: *A lunch break for the heavy unit: from left to right, Glast, Kettelhut, Bernhard, a troop doctor, Hst. Fritz Schröder, Luhmann.*

Now the hasty push to the east began. At the head of the German advance were the 2nd Battery and the Reconnaissance Unit, racing toward Melitopol. The battery chronicler portrayed: "Almost every day we had to deal with grotesque situations. Here is one of many examples: Our marching group is enveloped in swirling dust clouds. The encircling dust, which constantly infiltrates every cut and gap in our uniforms, down to our boots, with a fine layer, envelops the entire column concealingly.

"Into these advancing columns of dust there often come Russian trucks, mostly of the "SYS" brand. Coming out of side roads, they presume that it is a big column. Their surprise is all the greater when they learn during a pause that they are traveling with the Leibstandarte. After the initial shock they realize at once that flight is impossible. Without defending themselves, they let themselves be captured and disarmed. We immediately integrate the captured vehicles into our marching group, to replace lost vehicles as nearly as possible. Soviet supply vehicles also drive unsuspecting into our columns from the east and are taken. Vehicles that try to flee are brought to a stop after a short exchange of shots. And Panzermeyer's moving column does not stop. These events are part of our everyday life and no longer excite anyone. If someone had told us that months ago, it would have been rejected as a dream."

Before Neu-Stuttgart the 2nd Battery fired on groups of enemy armored vehicles. Children speaking Swabian begged for bread. Berdyansk on the Sea of Azov was reached. When the folloewing batteries and the staff of the I. Unit reached the city, the news spread among the people like wildfire. Alexander Sukkau, Sturmbannführer and Unit Commander, was born here on April 20, 1904. As the son of a German business representative, he spent his childhood in Berdyansk. The news that the later Marshal G. K. Zhukov was said to be Sukkau's stepbrother stubbornly made the rounds. It was made harder because the townspeople's conversations with Sukkau were listened in on. "Zhukov passed through here just a few days ago.") Despite his efforts, the chronicler could neither affirm nor refute the rumor.

On October 8, 1941 Mariupol was captured. In Mariupol the 2nd Battery;s guns were used in direct fire at the shortest range. Although howitzers, because of their design as high-angle guns, are not suited to direct fire, they were used more and more for unforeseen purposes.

The LAH artillerymen use their guns in every situation. Almost all the gunners had had the enemy right ahead of their guns and pinpointed them at least once. The men at the howitzers saw the effects of the shells they fired. This strengthened their [p. 69] self-esteem and willingness to take risks. The gunners had respect and esteem for their guns. They knew exactly what they could accomplish in time of need. That created calm and confidence. The marching speed was increasingly delayed by 'balkas', long narrow gullies. They usually angled across the line of march. In October the autumn is already quite far along. The German Army is under pressure of time! The Leibstandarte pushed forward alone again. The troops cannot take it easy. The Mius river was crossed before Taganrog. Heavy Russian artillery fire fell on the crossing place and approach roads. Rolling attacks of Soviet bombers and fighters caused losses. Before Taganrog several armored vehicles also turned up and took the troops under fire east of the crossing place.

Battery Officer (Lohse), Ammunition Squad Leader (Bartsch, +) and Platoon Leader (Meyer) of the 2nd Battery tensely observe a dive-bomber attack.

A gun of the 2nd Battery fires directly on nests of Soviet resistance in the streets of Mariupol on October 8, 1941.

Sturmmann Meyer of a heavy howitzer battery told of an experience: "Right behind the guns we put up our four-man tents. Gunners Albrecht and Riese, as usual, mounted their machine guns on anti-aircraft tripods. All the vehicles were put under the cover of a row of bushes. In front, parallel to the road, ran a driveway. As night fell, we withdrew into our tents to get some sleep.

"Toward morning, just as it began to get light, we were abruptly awakened by the sentries: 'Alarm! The Ivans are coming!' In a moment we were up, looking around in amazement. Truck after truck, loaded with Red Army men, rode past on the road from right to left—25 meters from our gun barrels! Then shots fell to the left in the morning mist. The last three trucks stopped. The Soviets quickly jumped off and rushed toward us. Now things got going. We opened rapid fire from pistols, carbines and machine guns. After a few minutes the fight was over. All the attackers had fallen. The Russian trucks were shot up like sieves. Fortunately we only had to deal with the end of the enemy column. After all, we were only forty men strong. Then our comrades from the supply train came rushing up. The Russians had driven over their toes. Correctly, they had hidden in the bushes and had not been seen. Kitchen Chief Sabbatke said: "You can be glad that the goulash cannon was not damaged!' Then we heard that the column had encountered the security lines of the 13th Armored Division and had been wiped out."

A Soldier's Fate in the Artillery Regiment

SS Rottenführer Hermann Juhls (right), with Erich Meyer, formed a radio troop in the 1st Battery. They were together since the battery was formed in 1939. Juhls was also the driver of the radio car.

On October 15, 1941 the position of the 1st Battery was under heavy enemy fire all day. Since several vehicles had already been hit, Sturmmann Schrei of the repair troop was also up front. Juhls' troop was also utilized there. Erich Meyer received the order from Intelligence Officer Auge (at right) to bring new batteries up from behind.

At this time the radio car received a direct hit. The shell rolled under the abdomen of the Rottenführer at the wheel and shattered him. Those present still remember the horror of it. Hermi Juhls was fully conscious. "Tell my mother that I am thinking of her at this moment," those were his last words. Several nearby men were wounded by shell fragments, including the intelligence squad leader Wilhelm Auge and telephone man Erich Lemm. Richard Schrei, standing right beside the car, was very lucky. Only his dented steel helmet flew off his head, leaving slight scratches on the nape of his neck.

Suspecting nothing, Erich Meyer came to the site later and saw the horror. Just after this picture was taken, the earth was shaken by salvo fire ("Stalin Organs"), this time without losses.

On October 17, 1941 the LSSAH battalions attacked Taganrog from 5:30 A.M. on. At first the attack progressed well. The II. Battalion had already crossed the Taganrog-Rostov railway line by 8:15 A.M.. The strengthened III. Battalion (Frey), advancing in the front line with the 12tn and 13th Companies, had to cross open country in view of the enemy. At 10:15 three armored trains approached from Taganrog. One of them turned onto the Rostov line and was stopped by an antitank gun. The Frey Battalion had just crossed the track with the Pinter (12) and Olboeter (13) Companies at that time. The 11th Company (Jochen Peiper) was following closely when the other two armored trains drove into the middle of the two companies. The open country, cut only by a few ditches, offered no cover. The III. Battalion suffered very heavy losses. More than eighty men died in the fire of the armored trains.

One antitank gun was able to bring the locomotive of the first train to a stop about 600 meters north of the bend in the track. The second train thus had to stop about at the bend. A five-hour battle for the armored trains began. One train was shot up by the 8.8 cm guns of the 7th Battery. Another was destroyed by the fire of the 1st Battery.

In the process, Unterscharführer Hans Zagar, leader of a light howitzer platoon, performed determined and cold-blooded action. At once he brought a gun forward to be readied for firing behind a bush. The gunners hastily pushed the lFH 18 forward and fired on the train. Shot after shot came from the open firing position. The armored couplings were finally hit by armor-piercing shells. VB Radioman Meyer lay in the dead angle of the armored train, right before the roadbed. He still remembers the tense hours, alone and full of uncertainly. After the fighting around Taganrog ended, the Commander of the Leibstandarte appeared at the 1st Battery. He thanked his artillerymen for their action and gave Zagar the Iron Cross 1st Class. The whole gun crew was given the Iron Cross II.

Heavy rains made the roads and paths barely passable. Overnight the dust had turned to tough mud. Every movement became misery. This caused a crisis for the supply situation. For several days the troop was left on its own. Bad-weather columns were set up, with tracked vehicles, tractors and wagons. The LSSAH prepared to defend itself on the steppe.

The cars of the crewmen of the armored train taken under fire by the 1st Battery (Zagar) near Taganrog was partly burned out.

The Heavy Guns of the Artillery Regiment

A Heavy Howitzer 18 (barrel length 4.44 meters) of the II. Unit covers the advance of a horsedrawn Army division on the eastern front, autumn 1941.

The tractor is towing a gun of the Cannon Battery over a critical spot in the terrain in October 1941. The 10 cm cannon could fire shells as far as 19 kilometers. The barrel was 5.46 meters long. Thus a gap in the LSSAH Artillery Regiment was filled.

Members of the unit staff, at left the diarist, Hans Böttger, stand in front of a typical command bus (that of Kdr. Sukkau).

One last gun fires directly on enemy columns at close range.

Taganrog is near at hand. But first the chief of the 1st Battery has to get his men across the Mius river.

The Doar gun of the Heberer (+) Battery fires! The impacts of the heavy 15-cm shells tore big holes in the Soviet defensive lines before Taganrog.

Light howitzers of the 1st Unit are in a firefight near Chekhov's birthplace.

Factories in Taganrog are burning. They were hit by fire of the 1st Battery, whose observer took these pictures.

Barrage Fire

An infantryman, Hans Komischke, told of these days: "With my machine gun and one man I had a position some 50 meters ahead of the front line to secure. The observation officer had set himself up well. The shear scope reached just over the wall, and at right he had a small niche for the phone. In back he could sit on a bench. A narrow, shallow ditch snaked along somewhat farther back. During the day the officer was up front, but in the evening he drew back.

"Then we occupied his place. In those days it was relatively quiet, but the nights were very dark. Behind us, the 4th Company of Hauptsturmführer Krocza was dug in. About 8:00 P.M. a radioman of the battery reported on the phone and asked: 'Do you want to hear the news?' He had a German station on the radio and linked us all together: the battery's firing position, the company's command post and our observation post. I replied: 'Yes, go ahead!' Then, from thousands of kilometers away, dance music sounded in my advanced post. For me that was an uncannily good feeling.

"Suddenly I heard chains rattling. What was that? Frightened, I dropped the receiver and thought: 'My God!—Tanks!'

"The sound of chains grew louder and louder, as if it were directly in front of my hill. I rang twice and was immediately connected with the firing position. I said only: 'Fire zone 17!' (barrage fire area). That was the closest fire zone to the hill. The observation officer had told me that before. Then the intelligence man said on the phone: 'Do you want to hear the shots?' In my excitement I said 'Yes,' and then I heard: 'First group fired, 2nd group fired, third...' I didn't hear any more because of the noise around me. The artillery thundered onto my hill, and I couldn't see or hear anything. I could only take full cover.

"After a short time the magic was over. Right after that the telephone rang. The familiar voice spoke: 'How are you? Everything in order?' I answered tersely: 'Yes, all is well.' I didn't know what had happened. Everything went so fast, with immediate firing. After a short time, our unforgotten commander, Sturmbannführer Fritz Witt, came forward through the trench. He sat down behind my foxhole and said: 'You did a good job. You have the position farthest to the east. So you must pay close attention. Do you have anything to smoke?' I had nothing more. We smoked a cigar together and talked a while. Then he went back through the trench."

Lousebites and freezing decimated the units. At the beginning of November a cold spell began, with night temperatures to -20 C. Cannoneer Gottzmann's report shows how the cold and catastrophic road conditions affected the troops:

"In a pitch-black, bitter cold night we saw a luring fire on the horizon of an open field. We were drawn to the place as if by magic. We longed for warmth. The soldiers streamed in from al ldirections. When we took Taganrog, winter clothing from a Soviet depot had fallen into our hands. There were blue quilted jackets, felt boots and fur caps with the Soviet star on them. This star was replaced by the death's-head by us—though sometimes it wasn't. So externally we looked like Russians. The fire burned in one of three haystacks that someone had set afire. We stood around the fire and warmed ourselves half the night. Then we crawled into the other haystacks. Like bees in their hive we bored hole after hole in the hay. By the fire we had already noticed that there were more and more fur caps with Russian stars. It was striking, and we knew they were real Russians! But we were too weak and too tired to think about it. We had long since ceased to be surprised. We just slept beside each other. On the next morning we gathered our sleepers in and sent several dozen Red Army men westward. No shot fell, no hate came out. The cold had conquered us equally."

And Rostov remained unreachable before the troops. The poem expresses the mood of the time:

Before Rostov, November 1941

1. We lay before Rostov's gates
three weeks and even longer.
Was our homeland lost forever?
Am I myself a lost son?

2. France has been bitter enough,
but Russia is the devil's home.
No city, no pretty girl,
the landscape is bleak and unchanging.

3. We have dug ourselves in
two meters into a Russian field.
The mice scratch in the straw roof,
our pockets hold useless money.

4. The radiators are frozen,
no vehicle starts in the morning.
Our clothes and boots are tattered,
our hands are clammy and cold.

5. We've waited four weeks for mail,
we eat only dry bread.
Our bones are thoroughly rheumy,
and death flies over us.

6. To hell with cigarettes,
we smoke only Russian tea.
At home in featherbeds
lies the homeland army.

7. When a soldier takes his shirt off,
his heart is so heavy.
The gunshots never end, but
the lice grow more and more.

8. From the nightly sky there comes down
a spirit loaded with bombs.
It is 'Ivan the Russian scoundrel' who makes the eggs fall down.

9. And if everything is crappy,
that's how it has to be;
We grit our teeth and mutter:
'The Russians won't get us!'

An unknown soldier

Everywhere in the front area, signs point the way, whether to an ammunition dump or . . .

The NCOs are glad that the correct distance from Taganrog to Berlin-Lichterfelde is given on the sign.

A last service to the fallen comrade. The ammunition squad officer of the 2nd Battery, Hauptscharfürer Bartsch (sitting farthest back), fell on November 27, 1941 while leaving Rostov on the Don.

By the end of October 1941 the roads were roads of ice. The Leibstandarte is stuck in the frozen mud!

Attack on Rostov

On November 17, 1941 the attack in the direction of Rostov began after heavy artillery preparation by the Leibstandarte's batteries. In the afternoon hours of the next day the LSSAH reached the heavily occupied Krasny Krim. Hans Hartmann, gun leader in the 2nd Battery, remembers: "In the morning hours of November 19, 1941 the place was fired on by Russian artillery. The greatest part of the gun crew, including battery officer and platoon leaders, took cover in a cellar. I myself lay behind the wall of a house. Stairs, closed off above and below by doors, led to the cellar. Unfortunately, the entrance was in the direction of the enemy gunfire. Another problem was that the battery fired shells with delayed fuzes. We artillerymen know that. The shells detonated only part of a second after they hit.

"A shot penetrated the lower door and detonated in the cellar, where there were some 15 men of the gun crew. Three men who were nearest to the spot had their bodies filled with most of the shell fragments. Gunner Scheffler and Sturmmänner Gedicke and Jakob were killed. Horst Jakob lost both arms and legs, but he was fully conscious. 'Greet my Silesian home from me...' were his last words, which made us shudder. Then he was loaded into an ambulance and died on the way to the dressing station. We could not bury him ourselves. He lies under Russian soil somewhere on the road to Taganrog. No stone, nothing at all, remembers this worthy young man."

The cannon battery of the Leibstandarte experienced their blackest day at Krasny Krim on November 19, 1941. The Targeting NCO I (RI), Unterscharführer Sauter, reported:

"In the early morning hours we moved our position to Krasny Krim. About 1 km ahead of the place the battery, on the march, met with a penetrating strong Russian unit. We were able to set up two guns and drive the Soviets away with handguns. Then some 60 men of our 8th Battery had to gather in an open field. The cannons were soon shot down by antitank fire. There were many losses to artillery and machine-gun fire. When our ammunition was almost used up and scarcely a gunner was unwounded, four assault guns under Untersturmführer Isecke appeared to save us. Peiper's 11th Company strengthened our formation. Some tanks of the Army Tank Regiment 4 could be summoned by radio."

Before the attack on Rostov on November 20, 1941: the staff battery of the light unit, with Uscha. Poluschni.

"With the tanks we attacked the Russians. They soon offered no more resistance. The cannon battery had eleven men slightly wounded, the Peiper Company fifteen, and the tanks brought in 1100 prisoners. But along with many other comrades, Oberscharführer Walter (VB), Dr. Schönberg and a platoon leader had fallen." At 11:20 on November 20, 1941, the battalions set out to attack Rostov. The airfield was taken. Heberer's heavy howitzer battery went into position at the edge of the airfield. Russian positions on the north edge of the city, strengthened by antitank guns, were overwhelmed. From noon on the battalions were involved in bitter street warfare. The further penetration to the center of town was supported splendidly by the advanced howitzers of the 1st Battery. Hauptsturmführer Fritz Teufel gave an example of bravery and readiness for action. At the head of his 1st Battery, he stormed through the streets with the infantry, firing his carbine. Along with regular Red Army troops, factory guards, firemen and partisans went into battle against the Leibstandarte. After Hein Springer and his commando group had taken the Great Don Bridge, connections with the battalions could be established. But the positions on the Don could not be held by the worn-out units, since the Red Army sent strong forces into a counterattack. The III. Armored Corps was to be cut off. With strong fighter-plane units and following Stalin-organ fire, the Russians attacked. The main push was against the LSSAH positions, especially the reconnaissance unit. With the help of all the heavy weapons, all the attacks were beaten back. After a breakthrough by the 60th Infantry Division, a retaking of the front was ordered.

The III. Battalion, while leaving the position near Leninovan on November 28, encountered a T-34 pack, which was turned back by an AR-LSSAH battery. Their own artillery and splendidly flown dive-bomber attacks held the enemy down again. The LSSAH was ordered to defend itself in the Szambek position. While unloading in the early hours of December 1, all the tanks and guns had to be taken along. A strong attack struck the IV. Battalion on November 30. Only with the help of the immediately assigned tank destroyers, assault guns, and the 1st Battery could the battle group, taken over by Obersturmbannführer, hang on.

From December 1, 1941 on, the LSSAH units began to separate from the enemy and march into the Szambek position en masse. Very limited by the enemy, one company per battalion took up an intercepting position. The artillery looped backward to support the defensive combat with two units. Teufel's battery remained with Witt's group. While unloading, the 1st Battery had to turn aside to an intermediate position under direct Russian fire. One T-34 tank was shot down.

The Battery Chief of the I./SS-AA "LSSAH", Hauptsturmführer Teufel (+), with his deputy and successor, Obersturmführer Gladoss (+), are seen during a pause in battle in the streets of Rostov.

The 1st Battery in the Streets of Rostov on the Don

The howitzers fire on Russian defenses at point-blank range.

Fired! The gun crew is seen as the smoke rises. After firing, the gun barrel recoils.

The 1st Battery in the short phase of the intermediate position after leaving Rostov on the Don on December 1, 1941.

Winter Positional War on the Szambek

For the first time in this war, the troops did not move into warm, dry quarters. After the engineers had blown holes in the hard-frozen earth, bunkers and foxholes were built. A six-month winter positional war began. Again and again, Russian units touched the main battle line and had to be taken under fire. The guns were overworked and could be repaired only with difficulty. With their worn-out barrels, the 2nd Battery could not hit a Russian railway despite a good view. The shots were simply too scattered.

On December 19m 1941 the Artillery Regiment lost one of its best men, as well as the future Unit Commander. Hauptscharführer Wilhelm Auge recalled:

"On this day I, as intelligence squad leader of the 1st Battery, was at the observation post with our chief, Hauptsturmführer Teufel. Russian artillery fired on us. The shells fell close to us. Hauptsturmführer Teufel collapsed beside me. He had been wounded mortally on the head by a shell fragment. In my next furlough I visited his widow in Frankfurt on the Oder. I brought some personal belongings and told her of the battles."

Hauptsturmführer Teufel was buried in Taganrog on December 20, 1941. All of the transport units took part in the burial. The 2nd Battery, in their position up front, fired a salute in his honor. The shells flew over to the Russians.

Für Führer und Volk starb
im Osten den Heldentod der
SS-Standartenführer
Fritz Teufel
SS-Hstuf. u. Batteriechef in der
Waffen-SS
Inhaber des EK. I. u. II. Klasse.
ᛉ 27. 7. 1907 ᛦ 19. 12. 1941
Sein ganzes Leben war Kampf für
seinen Führer und sein Volk.
Emma Teufel, geb. Lieb, und
Kinder **Ursel** und **Volker**.
Frankfurt/Oder, Weinbergweg 31.

The death notice in the Black Corps of April 2, 1942.

Erich Meyer, VB radioman in the 1st Battery, reported on the positional war:

"Our advanced observer, Unterscharführer Alois Plattner, was badly wounded by a shot in the lung. Because of the enemy's position we could not move him out at first. Only during the night did we rescue Plattner alive. After being in the hospital, he returned to us." Unfortunately, Hauptscharführer Alois Plattner fell near Caen in July 1944.

A bad case of sabotage happened to the 1st Battery. Wilhelm Auge observed: "When we fired a light howitzer shell we had a bore explosion. That means that the shell exploded in the gun barrel right after firing. The barrel was torn apart. The effect was horrible. All those at the gun were killed instantly."

The chronicler of the 1st Unit, Hans Böttger, reported that the gun crew all had their heads blown off. The case was investigated carefully and traced back to the ammunition factory. Other manipulated ammunition was found by the 1st Battery. At the last second, further destruction could thus avoided.

The 5th Battery took up a position on a slope some 3 kilometers west of the village of Szambek. The places for the guns were chosen very favorably by Obersturmführer Heberer. There was a former sheep farm there with a cottage and a destroyed manger. A deep well with a winch, chain and bucket was also a stroke of luck. The best trinking and washing water was always available. Heberer, already an artilleryman in World War I, acted very sensibly and cautiously. Guns and ammunition supplies were covered with linen cloths. The nightly sentries had to wipe out their footprints at dawn with twig brooms. Every unnecessary movement was omitted. A 'balka' behind the firing position could not be used to build a bunker, since it was marked on maps. Sooner or later the Russians would fire on it. Heberer had a wealth of tricks and artifices in other ways too.

At the end of May 1942, the Leibstandarte was withdrawn from the front. Parts of the Artillery Regiment remained in their old positions until June 12, 1942. After a time in the Mariupol-Stalino area, they were sent by rail to France for refreshment as of July 11, 1942. Because of a command change in the I. Unit, the light batteries were put into a hollow square. Kurt Frentrupp has a bitter memory of that:

"While inspecting the new front, the new Unit Commander Steineck noticed that almost all those in our 2nd Battery wore the wound emblem. That was obviously not right as he saw it. He gave the order that in the future the wound decoration should only be given when he thought the wound was bad enough. We were very hurt.

"In the end we had almost 60 wounded men, and had lost over 90 in the campaigns since France. Steineck, formerly Commander of the Heavy Battalion (infantry guns and tank destroyers), had as yet learned nothing of the fighting style of light artillery by fast troops. When he saw that everything was done properly, he canceled this stupid order."

The 5th Battery (heavy howitzer), Artillery Regiment, LSSAH, in its 1941-42 winter position.

Losses of the 2nd Battery, AR-LSSAH, from July to December 1941

This incomplete list was based on diary notes. Columns: name; SS rank; killed (+); badly wounded (++); wounded (+++); date; place; cause; and return to unit [ja = yes, nein = no].

Schütte	Mann	+++	14. 7. 41	Dolczyk	Inf.	ja
Saul	Ost.	++	27. 7. 41	Sokolowka	Ari	nein
Stein	Mann	+++	08/1941	?	Ari	ja
Fleckenstein	Strm.	+++	08/1941	?	Ari	ja
Hörens	Strm.	+++	08/1941	?	Ari	ja
Reinelt	Strm.	+++	08/1941	?	Inf.	ja
Bolz	Mann	+++	08/1941	?	Flugz.	ja
Wöllke	Mann	+++	08/1941	?	Ari	ja
Klimke	Strm.	+	16. 8. 41	Sasselje	Ari	-
Kirchhof	Mann	+	16. 8. 41	Sasselje	Ari	-
Kuka	Mann	+	16. 8. 41	Sasselje	Ari	-
Krause	Uscha.	+++	16. 8. 41	Sasselje	Ari	ja
Pabst	Uscha.	+++	16. 8. 41	Sasselje	Ari	ja
Hartmann	Strm.	+++	16. 8. 41	Sasselje	Ari	ja
Kröss	Strm.	++	16. 8. 41	Sasselje	Ari	nein
Müller	Strm.	+++	16. 8. 41	Sasselje	Ari	ja
Cischek	Hst.	++	17. 8. 41	Sasselje	Unfall mitWaffe	nein
Schmidt	Strm.	+	19. 8. 41	Cherson	Ari	-
Kaiser	Mann	+	19. 8. 41	Cherson	Ari	-
Dinter	Uscha.	+++	19. 8. 41	Cherson	Ari	ja
Krause	Strm.	+++	19. 8. 41	Cherson	Ari	ja
Frentrup	Mann	+++	19. 8. 41	Cherson	Ari	ja
Boltze	Mann	+++	13. 9. 41	Preobrashenka	Ari	ja
Arens	Mann	+	16. 9. 41	Genitschesk	Inf.	-
Mutterlose	Strm.	++	16. 9. 41	Genitschesk	Inf.	nein
Müller	Oscha.	+++	09/1941	Genitschesk	Ari	ja
Fuss	Mann	+++	09/1941	Genitschesk	Ari	ja
Friedrich	Uscha.	+	24. 9. 41	Preobrashenka	Ari	-
Kirschner	Strm.	+	24. 9. 41	Preobrashenka	Ari	-
Ohst	Strm.	++	24. 9. 41	Preobrashenka	Ari	nein
Johann	Mann	+++	27. 9. 41	Preobrashenka	Flugz.	ja
Custas, Dr.	Ost.	+++	09/1941	Preobrashenka	Ari	ja
Mahron	Strm.	+	8. 10. 41	Mangusch	Flugz.	-
Mück	Strm.	+	8. 10. 41	Mangusch	Flugz.	-
Scholz	Mann	+	8. 10. 41	Mangusch	Flugz.	-
Schreck	Mann	+	8. 10. 41	Mangusch	Flugz.	-
Thuminger	Mann	+	8. 10. 41	Mangusch	Flugz.	-
Heldt	Strm.	+++	8. 10. 41	Mangusch	Flugz.	ja
Lütje	Strm.	+++	8. 10. 41	Mangusch	Flugz.	ja
Giebitz	Strm.	+++	10/1941	?	eigene Flak	ja
John	Strm.	+++	12. 10. 41	Nikolajewka	Ari	ja
Knapp	Strm.	+++	12. 10. 41	Nikolajewka	Ari	ja
Gebhardt	Mann	++	12. 10. 41	Nikolajewka	Ari	nein
Hoffmann	Strm.	+++	10/1941	?	Ari	ja
Dinter	Uscha.	+++	10/1941	?	Ari	ja
Hüsken	Uscha.	++	24. 10. 41	Mogila	Flugz.	nein
Liebich	Strm.	+++	24. 10. 41	Mogila	Flugz.	ja
Nau	Strm.	++	24. 10. 41	Mogila	Flugz.	ja
Ploch	Strm.	++	28. 10. 41	Mogila	Ari	nein
Riedel	Strm.	+++	11/1941	?	Inf.	ja
Herbruck	Oscha.	+++	11/1941	?	Inf.	ja
Gedicke	Strm.	+	19. 11. 41	Krasnij Krim	Ari	-
Jakob	Strm.	+	19. 11. 41	Krasnij Krim	Ari	-
Scheffler	Mann	+	19. 11. 41	Krasnij Krim	Ari	-
Czaupa	Uscha.	+++	19. 11. 41	Krasnij Krim	Ari	-
Dinter	Uscha.	+++	19. 11. 41	Krasnij Krim	Ari	ja
Rossbert	Mann	+++	19. 11. 41	Krasnij Krim	Ari	ja
Bartsch	Hscha.	+	27. 11. 41	Ssernikoff	Ari	ja
Golz	Strm.	+++	29. 11. 41	Tschaltyr	Flugz.	-
Mannek	Uscha.	+++	07. 12. 41	Ssambek	Flugz.	ja
Nispel	Mann	+++	07. 12. 41	Ssambek	Flugz.	ja
Arendt	Mann	+++	12/1941	Ssambek	Ari	ja

Obersturmführer Victor Gladoss, successor to the late Hauptsturmführer Teufel as Chief of the 1st Battery.

A system of deep trenches came into being. Untersturmführer Helmut Henssler was transferred to the 2nd Battery as observation officer after Helmut Haak had to be sent to the 1st Battery.

Sturmmann Knapp is disturbed by enemy fire at dawn and looks uneasily out of the trench.

Observation with a shear scope: The enemy attack broke down under the fire of a nearby Army mortar battery, with very heavy losses among the Red Army men.

The firing positions of the 2nd Battery were in an open field, where the guns were dug in. The gunners stood in the icy, stinging cold in insufficient winter clothing.

Nailed boots were the best conductors of coldness. Whoever had no captured felt boots was well advised to wrap canvas or sacks around his feet. There were also supply problems. Artillery ammunition came through only in small quantities.

The observatioon posts were under constant artillery fire and could be left only at night. The advanced observers, such as Uscha. Rothe of the 3rd Battery, had rough times.

Bunker cave-ins were brought on by damp weather. The 4th Battery lost four men that way. The bunkers were strengthened by additional stabilizing. Smoke and air pipes rise from a bunker of the 1st Battery here.

Mail call! The men of the 3rd Battery are visibly glad that their long-awaited mail has arrived at last.

Hans Krahn of the Intelligence Squad of the 1st Battery enjoys his fried eggs in the bunker. A record player helps to pass the time. The 2nd Battery also had music to enjoy. A shellac record with the song of the worklng class was found. This record was always put on when the guns were firing. Along with their thunder the Internationale could be played!

A soldier's letter

Excerpts from a letter by Rottenführer Gerd Friedrich (died 1944), 1st Clerk, 2nd Battery, AR-LSSAH, addressed to Sturmmann Mutterlose, formerly telephone man in that battery. He looked forward to recovering from serious wounds in Germany.

In the east, January 15, 1942
Dear Horst!

After long waiting and worrying, we finally received a sign of life from you, your long letter of December 4, 1941. Most hearty thanks!

Now you have reached a hospital in Germany. I am wondering when we will see our Fatherland again?! I rejoice with you in the love that the homeland lets every wounded man be a part of. With such treatment it will be no wonder if you gain weight at once.

The 2nd Battery is still the "old heap". But death has taken many from our ranks, and we have lost several badly wounded men too.

On the Crimean isthmus on September 24, 1941 we lost Uscha. Friedrich and Sturmmann Kirschner. Sturmmann Ohst was wounded. On the morning of October 8, 1941, Rata attacks took Sturmmann Marohn, Mück, Cannoneer Scholz, Schreck and Thuminger. Sturmmann Heldt, who is back with the battery, was wounded. On October 12 an armored platoon clobbered us before Taganrog. Sturmmann John, Cannoneer Knapp and Gebhardt were wounded. In the battles at Rostov a direct artillery hit on a cellar took Sturmmann Jakob, Gedicke and Scheffler. Jakob died in transport; both his arms and legs were blown off. In a night bomb attack before Rostov—we were in a field—a direct hit landed between the kitchen and another truck (Russian 3-ton). Unterscharführer Hüsken was so badly wounded that he lost a leg. Sturmmann Nau's right arm was smashed. Two days later, Sturmmann Ploch was so badly wounded by a shell fragment at the observation post that he also lost a leg. On November 27, 1941, Hauptscharführer Bartsch took a shell fragment in the head some eight kilometers beyond Rostov. His poor wife! But their four-month-old daughter Karin will console her in her sorrow. During the withdrawal from Rostov an air attack wounded Sturmmann Golz. Bartsch's grave was flattened to ground level to avoid desecration.

Sturmmann Fleckenstein, Landgraf, Kirsten and Gründel, who were on your vehicle when it was attacked, have returned to the battery and sent you their hearty greetings.

The battery is presently in firing position in an open field. Well-built bunkers are its barracks, but there is no water anywhere nearby. The observation post is in a village that is constantly under artillery fire. One can leave the post only at night. Thus once a week five men come to the supply depot and get a little rest.

As for your return, I have already talked with the Staff Scharführer. I promise you I'll do everything in my power to have you return to us.

I wish you a good recovery and "Auf Wiedersehen!" soon.

Hearty greetings from

Your Comrade Gerd

Long-Distance Marriage in the Field

Above: *Early in 1942 the Telephone Troop Leader Schumacher (1st Battery) was married in Taganrog.* Below: *The wedding is recorded by the Unit Commander (Sukkau).*

For the ceremony, the battery stood in formation, flanked by two guns. The city children's home can be seen in the background. The light howitzers of th 1st Battery bear tank-kill rings.

Only a few meters from the shore of the Sea of Azov, the guns stand in formation.

After the ceremony ends, Unterscharführer Hopfner satands before his victorious lFH 18 gun.

Above: *Officers and NCO of the 1st Battery stand for a group photo. In the center is Ost. Gladoss (Chief), Staff Scharführer Küspert (6th from right, Ust. Haak (5th from left), Hscha. Auge (3rd from left).* Below: *Rail transport to France after a year of action on the eastern front. The officers play skat. Steineck (center) took over the light unit from Sukkau.*

The grave of Wenzel Kirschner, who died in Crimea on September 25, 1941.

The many graves of the dead were left behind. Alfred Hansel, Leader of the 3rd Battery, died on November 27, 1941.

The Leibstandarte on Parade in Paris

Above: *Field Marshal Gerd von Rundstedt reviews the parade on the Avenue des Champs-Elysees, along with the Division Commander, Obergruppenführer Sepp Dietrich, as Commander, West.* Below: *The Unit Commander of the I./SS-AR "LSSAH" heads toweard the Arc de Triomphe.*

Above: *The Commander's car is followed by that of the Chief of the 1st Battery with the photographer, Hauptscharführer Wilhelm Auge, in the passenger's seat.* Below: *Obersturmführer Eisse de Vries, Battery chief of the 1st Battery, is seen before entering the chief's car. At the Jelna bend de Vries, Battery Leader of the artillery regiment "Das Reich," was badly wounded. After his recovery he joined the Leibstandarte.*

The motorcycle couriers of de Vries' battery are seen on the grand boulevard of Paris.

Untersturmführer Schulz, Unit Adjutant of the I./ SS-AR "LSSAH", is seen during the parade day. Josef Schulz fell in the street fighting at Kharkov on March 12, 1943.

An 8-ton medium towing tractor, Sd.Kfz. 7 (III. Unit) on the Champs-Elysees, carrying the crew of a heavy howitzer (7 cannoneers, gun leader and driver).

Refreshing in Northern France

Above: *The Artillery Commander of the Leibstandarte awaits its Division Commander. All the artillery regiment commanders are in this photo: Staudinger (until May 1943) at left, then Mertsch as Commander of the Heavy Unit (Staudinger's successor), and Steineck (3rd from left) as Commander of the I. Unit (Mertsch's successor as of June 1944).* Below: *"Guard—Halt!" Rottenführer Mülln (Pay clerk, 1st Battery) is on duty at the outer gate.*

Above: *The Commander's big Mercedes has arrived. Walter Staudinger reports to Sepp Dietrich. Unterscharführer Fellhölter stands guard at the gate.*
Below: *Generaloberst Curt Haase, Commander of the 15th Army, inspects the 1st Battery of the Leibstandarte on August 10, 1942, along with the Division and Regimental Commanders.*

Above: *Haase, an old artilleryman, is especially interested in the gun drills. After the Generaloberst left the LAH, Eisse de Vries (left) was ordered to the division's command post. There Sepp Dietrich praised the 1st Battery and gave good wishes to the Battery Chief and his men.* Below: *After the inspection, the Division Commander awarded decorations. Unterscharführer Stoffers, medic of the 1st Battery, received the Iron Cross II. Sepp Dietrich is accompanied by the 1st General Staff Officer, Obersturmbannführer Wilhelm Keilhaus (who bore the German Cross in gold since April 29, 1942).*

While Obergruppenführer Dietrich pins the Iron Cross I on a Hauptsturmführer, Richard Schrei of the 1st Battery's Repair Troop takes pictures.

He was sternly scolded by the officers standing around, and told to disappear at once. Sepp Dietrich noticed and was the only one to stand up for him. "Let the boy take pictures!" smiled the unforgettable Commander at the camera. Almost every LAH soldier had his own very personal meeting with Sepp Dietrich to remember.

Above: *Walter Staudinger awards further decorations and symbols of honor. He himself wears both the Iron Cross I and the Bulgarian Military Order (eight-pointed white cross, Bulgarian lion in the medallion, with crossed swords) for bravery in the war. Besides the German Cross in gold (since June 18, 1942), he held the Order of the Star of Romania.* Below: *In conclusion, the War Service Cross and Iron Cross II are awarded by the Regimental Commander.*

Sturmbannführer Gustav Mertsch presents the heavy unit, which has marched up, to the Regimental Commander.

Sepp Dietrich with his artillerymen. In the background are the battery chiefs of all the units of the regiment (2nd from right, Wilhelm Preuss, Commander of the SS Corps Artillery Unit 101 in 1944-45; see pp. 200-201).

Fritz Kurzendorfer (+) makes music in Nonancur. At left sits Heinz Lorenz (1st Battery), who fell as SS Untersturmführer in Hungary on March 21, 1945. With the last "Wasp" he covered the withdrawal in the face of strong armored units.

Only once was the calm broken by the Canadian landing in Dieppe. All LAH units—here the 1st Battery—were in alarm readiness on August 19, 1942.

NCO training took place in France. Here Unterscharführer Klimatschek conducts gun training with an lFH 18 howitzer.

The Panoramic Scope 32! Because of the addition of newly-formed batteries (three light, two heavy, one launcher), the Artillery Regiment grew to include 12 batteries. The former Flak Battery (6./7. AR) became the cadre of the LAH Flak Unit.

3

The Battle for Kharkov

After the 6th Army (Paulus) was surrounded in Stalingrad, the Soviets prepared for their next advance to the Don and Tchir. It encountered the 8th Italian Army, whose entire front was torn up. The Italians were in a steady retreat.

The Soviet armies pushed far to the west and threatened Rostov.

Thus the SS Armored Grenadier Division "LSSAH" had to gather in the area southeast of Kharkov in such a manner that they could be utilized as quickly as possible to secure the Donetz sector between Smiyev and Khotomlya. The Division was subordinated to the SS Armored Corps of Hausser.

The Leibstandarte had been getting loaded up since January 11, 1943. The batteries of the artillery regiment were issued one 5 cm antitank gun per battery for this action. On January 22, 1943 the advance command arrived, assigning the position areas on and east of the Donetz. Seven days later, after a train trip of barely ten days, the first units arrived in the new combat area southeast of Kharkov. The 1st Battery was unloaded as part of the first transport group. Along with the reconnanssance unit and the 4th Battery, it was sent directly from the unloading depot to its positions. The new Battery Chief of the 1./AR-LSSAH, Obersturmführer Eisse de Vries, reported: "Units moving the other way, flowing backward, made a powerless and demoralizing impression. They looked at us wide-eyed. At the Donetz, enemy attacks were repulsed, some with direct fire of our guns. At the beginning of February, after returning from the advanced observer, I determined that our own unloading movements were in progress. I went forward again and brought the observer and radioman back."

The 11th Battery with their heavy howitzers were one of the last LSSAH units to reach the Donetz. Here the division was in defensive action at support points on both side of Tchuguyev. They defended a sector of the front of about 100 kilometers! Providing sufficient artillery support to all the applied forces was impossible. The individual batteries were pulled far apart and assigned or subordinated to the involved units. A unified front could not be formed with the available forces. The overextended situation of the division was clear to see. The encirclement of Kharkov was in progress.

Rail transport to Tchuguyev. A Flak machine gun protects the staff battery from low-flying plane attacks. Astonishing success was attained against IL-2 and Yak planes. Thus Sturmmann Hofbauer (launcher) was able to shoot down two planes from the end of the train.

Very superior enemy forces attacked the 1st SS Regiment near Rogan from February 10 on. There was bitter fighting. In this sector was the newly introduced Do-launcher battery, which contributed considerably to the defensive success with their surface fire. The de Vries Battery was also there; thechief of the 1st Battery made a dramatic report on the situation at the Rogan railway station. Here the enemy broke through the Weidenhaupt Battalion's lines north of the Rogan depot at 11:10 A.M. on February 14, 1943. Eisse de Vries wrote: "At the first light the Russians attacked our positions with loud screams. In great haste we brought the guns forward and brought the enemy down with direct fire. Sturmbannführer Max Hansen subordinated the heavy infantry guns to me. Along with our howitzers we formed a porcupine; the gun barrels were its quills. Next to us the Russians marched through. Our link with the Weidenhaupt Battalion was lost. We fought off all attacks. As often before, the attack area before our position was strewn with fallen Russians. The Russians were behind us, yet the "Rogan depot position" was held by us!" The 19-year-old Untersturmführer Gerd Noack, advanced observer and observation officer, fell in his first action with the 1st Battery.

Hard fighting took place all day on February 15, 1943, on the railway line and at the tractor works. In the evening the units received orders from the SS Armored Corps to withdraw, so as to avoid being encircled. The route back across the deep gully of the Udy Brook caused much difficulty because of the ice-covered roads and paths. What problems had to be overcome can be seen in the description by an assault-gun commander (Jäckel): "In the night we set off. It was bitterly cold. Stop, go, stop, go, so it went all night. Then came the Udy, and at the edge of the road we saw wildly shouting and waving soldiers. I stopped my assault gun and asked what was wrong. The broken-down tractor of their 10-cm cannon was towed away, but the recovery vehicle could not tow the gun. They asked if we couldn't take it along. Naturally they hooked the thing on and climbed onto my vehicle.

"Everything went very well as long as the road was level. When we approached the Udy crossing, that was to change. Steep descent to the bridge and steep ascent on the other side! In low gear the rig, assault gun and 10-cm cannon, crept slowly down the hill. The cannon pushed so hard that the assault gun's right track went into the roadside ditch. We tried to get back on the road, but in vain. So the whole rig drove on to the bridge in the ditch. At a flat place we got back out of the ditch. All went well over the bridge, but how would it go on the steep upgrade? The road was smooth ice. So we approached with verve, shifted down, and then everybody got out. Whether assault-gun man or cannoneer, everybody pushed: 24 tons of assault gun plus the towed 10-cm cannon with limber (6.5 tons). It was really no flyweight! Almost at the top the tracks turned without gripping. Damned trouble! But other comrades came running and pushed with all their strength. We did it! On the next day the Commander of the Artillery Regiment thanked us by teletype for rescuing the crew and gun." The Red Army pushed ever nearer to Kharkov. At Merefa a reception line was set up for the returning troops.

On the march to the Donetz. Biting frost and icy roads hindered vehicle traffic. Winter camouflage has not yet been applied.

When Hausser's order to withdraw reached the troops, the 1st Battery was still far east of Kharkov. Eisse de Vries radioed the regiment from a hopeless position, asking permission to blow up the howitzers. Permission was given by Oberführer Staudinger. But it didn't come to that. The battery succeeded in a "horizontal sneak". The supply train was then at a schoolyard in Kharkov. Staff Scharführer Auge was instructed by radio to pack up at once. Richard Schrei of the repair troop recalled: "I just came from a Wehrmacht maintenance depot and could have improved our equipment a little. One lonely sentry stood guard there. I said to him: 'Man, see to it that you get out of here!' The retreat order has come!' He was completely baffled, and I had to persuade him to disappear. At night the battery came in from combat and we fell in at the end of the marching column. The drive through the evacuated and ghostly-looking city still remains in my mind. Our column was shot at by civilians. We were really happy to escape again."

The battery chief added: "In the withdrawal we covered the infantry's departure. We were the last motorized unit to drive through Kharkov at dawn. When we reached the reception line, completely exhausted, the Unit Adjutant Schulz greeted us. He could not share our feelings. For one thing, we were glad to escape, and for another, there was much bitterness about the withdrawal. For several days we had not slept and were physically done in. But there was no rest, for we had to go into position again at once. The rear guard's withdrawal was covered by firing fog grenades."

After the evacuation of Kharkov, the Leibstandarte was with various battle group southwest of town in varying offensive and defensive actions spread over extensive flatlands. A precise description of the fighting would smash the covers of the book, so that only a few battles will be described. During the battle for Kharkov, the LAH Launcher Battery first went into action with their 15-cm Do-foglayers. 18-year-old Wilfrid Ihle experienced his first front service here. He reported: "Our battery was very far behind the main battle line, surely 10 kilometers. During the entire winter combat at Kharkov we were sort of 'firemen". Whenever there was danger somewhere, we moved in lightning-fast. Then three salvos were fired and we moved on. The observation officer was Ust. Reinhold Macke.

Untersturmführer Karl-Heinz Protze was surrounded in Taranovka with the supply and ammunition troops of the 11th Battery. On February 17, 1943 the breakthrough to the battery took place. All the supply trucks, mainly Opel Blitz, and ammunition trucks fitted with chains ("Mulis") were lost. Worst of all, the kitchen and provision trucks with food and other goods, were gone.

Within ten seconds one launcher fired six rockets. Three salvos were fired in five minutes. One disadvantage, though, was the heavy smoke that developed after ignition. The black powder made a smoke like that of burning tires. In later use this could be improved. What remained was the plume, visible from afar, that betrayed us easily. Our launchers with their overwhelming flat fire were much feared by all enemies. They panicked quickly!

The rockets were packed individually. For the ammunition men it meant a lot to carry. A container plus contents weighed over 35 kilograms."

The 3rd Battery of Obersturmführer Helmut Haak fought along with Panzermeyer's reconnaissance unit and Max Wünsche's armored unit. From Yeremeyevka an armored advance to the southward was conducted. The support point of Yeremeyevka remained in the hands of the artillery and antitank forces. They used harassing fire to delude the enemy as to their real objectives. Panzermeyer wrote in his book "Grenadiere": "Leaving the support point was done unnoticed. The artillery directed harassing fire at known positions. Our marching group could hardly be seen in the deep snow. A long village took up the marching Russians. Enemy columns moved westward undisturbed. Should we venture to go after them?" The marching group was completely shattered and rolled up. On this February 21, 1943 the beloved battery chief of the 3,/AR-LSSAH, Helmut Hauk, fell. He was just hurrying after the commander of the strengthened Reconnaissance Unit when he met a Russian scouting troop. His successor, Obersturmführer Gille, was badly wounded at the same place shortly afterward.

After the enemy columns were wiped out, the strengthened AA attacked strong Red Army positions. Panzermeyer had the intention of leading his troops far to the north, then turn southeastward and break into the readiness positions near Nizhni-Orel.

Panzermeyer, in "Grenadiere", wrote: "The movements were to be carried out so that we would arrive behind the enemy at dawn. At this time, with cooperation from the artillery, all the supply drivers were to make a sham attack and attract the Russians' attention to the west.

"I gave the artillery in Yeremeyevka the command to fire. We all waited tensely for the first shots. The impacts would show whether we had approached the right place. Correct—just to our right. our howitzers were hammering the Russian position. Glaring flashes lit up the scene for us. The advanced artillery observer brought the fire together and directed it at our breakthrough position. We stood to the side of the impacts and could observe their effect precisely. Now the moment had come! Within an hour the village belonged to us. Our artillery created their masterpiece. Like an all-shattering fist, it plunged on before us. It was no wonder, for the observer was sitting amid the enemy." The Russians lost about 1000 men, several heavy batteries, antitank guns and ammunition stores. The assault hit the Russian command post squarely.

Horst Mutterlose of a heavy howitzer battery reported of the attack on Bereka: "The attack rolled on and we had to go farther forward. Sturmbannführer Mertsch, our unit commander, then said to me: 'Mutterlose, you and your men follow right after Hauptsturmführer Werner!' For our telephone men that was very laborious. We carried backpacks with field cable and telephone sets. Walking through knee-high snow, we fell farther and farther back despite all our efforts. When a Hiwi near us was wounded in the leg, we quickly put on a bandage. The distance to Commander Werner (II. Unit) grew farther and farther. A Balka moving across the direction of attack was another hindrance. While we struggled to cross the Balka, Werner was climbing out of it on the opposite bank. At that moment a heavy-caliber shell landed right next to the Hauptsturmführer and tore him down. When we arrived he was already dead. His adjutant, Untersturmführer Balschuweit, took care of him. Only much later did we learn that he was also wounded. The situation did not allow any burial at first. So Rottenführer Mika had his dead commander in his vehicle for two days. Dead or alive, every man took part in the attack."

Mutterlose gives another impressive report of the 11th (heavy howitzer) battery: "Early one afternoon the Ivans pulled a 'Ratsch-Bum" gun into position by hand. At once the grenadiers asked if we wanted to attack. Yes, of course, but the observer said that where one gun was, others would come. So we waited. Laboriously the Russians pulled a second gun up the slope. Four guns had been brought into position splendidly. Nothing had opposed us... Günther Nusche had already calculated the shot values. Ammunition distribution had been approved by the battery chief.

Graves of the 1st Unit, February 22-23, 1943: Obersturmführer Helmut Haak (Chief, 3rd Battery), Gunner Heinz Bahr, Untersturmführer Günther Kurth (Intelligence Officer and Chief of the Staff Battery).

Gunners of the Cannon Battery pose on a captured British "Matildä Mark II armored infantry gun, which had been delivered to the Red Army. By August 1943 almost 3000 "Matildas" had been built.

The observer gave the command to fire, I passed it on by phone to the firing position. Only moments later our heavy shells howled away. We had quickly zeroed in on the Russian all-purpose guns and went over to efficacious fire. The shots landed in the middle of their target. In a few minutes everything was over.

"In the same position, almost on the opposite height of the slope, was one of the typical limed huts of the area. In the early morning hours, the Russian telephone men laid a cable to the house. They moved completely secure and undisturbed. We were drooling, scarcely taking our telescopes from our eyes. Gradually a back-and-forth traffic to the house developed. A staff was set up there. This tempting behavior had to be punished. We had already zeroed in on various spots in the area. As we had homed in on the barrage-fire areas, we had determined shot values that we could use again. We had drawn an appropriate sketch map with clammy fingers. All the values were marked on it. So it was not difficult to direct our fire at that house. The first shots had a destructive effect on the target. Surprised Red Army men came jumping out the windows. A command post had thus been knocked out."

The Battery Chief, Obersturmführer Lehnert, achieved another master stroke of artillery near Olkhovatka (about 2/28/43). The 11th Battery's chronicler recorded it: "Russians with tanks had broken through near our 1st Armored Grenadier Regiment. From our observation post in a hay hut we could see that clearly. Our senses were wide awake at once. We saw clearly that the convoy was heading toward the village in which we had a firing position. We gave the alarm at once over the phone wires. The challenging situation was sized up well by our young battery chief. At once he had two heavy howitzers swung around 180 degrees from their original aiming positions. We were ready to fire again in no time. The tanks stopped when they saw the village, and some of the men got out. The first shots left our gun barrels. The first impacts showed clearly how precisely we had worked. They landed right between the Russian tanks. The halting place was taken under fire effectively. Our tenseness and excitement at the observation post changed to spreading relaxation. We saw how the tank crews jumped into the T-34 tanks in a panic. The truck crews tried to jump onto their vehicles. But for three tanks it was too late. One of them turned in a circle, as the track had been hit. Two antitank guns towed by the trucks could also be destroyed. Now our assault guns joined in and took part in the battle. The battery lost two men. The provision drivers had been hit. Not knowing the situation, they were on the way to the observation posts with their sleds and had encountered the tank breakthrough. Without firing a shot, they were mowed down by the tanks' machine guns."

Battle near Olkhovatka: 75 shots were fired at the Russian T-34 tanks. Empty cartridges indicate the hard work of the 11th Battery. The ramrod that pushed the heavy 15-cm shells into the gun barrel can be seen clearly.

Hooking up a Light Howitzer 18 of the 2nd Battery in the area south of Kharkov in February 1943.

Three of the Heavy Artillery Unit's six radiomen fell in action: Hild, Oeser (+), Kottenhahn, Lehmkühler (+), Hunold and Brobetzky (+).

Recapture of Kharkov

From March 4, 1943 on, the Leibstandarte was regrouped for an advance to the north. The Division pushed through the Msha sector, through a fully surprised enemy, into the area north of Kharkov. The 1st Battery belonged to the Peiper Battle Group, which consisted of the SPW Battalion, the Rettlinger Assault-gun Battery, and the Prinz Tank-destroyer Company. Eisse de Vries reported on outstanding cooperation. On March 11, 1943 the assault on Alexeyevka, barely two kilometers north of Kharkov, failed. The attack came to a standstill. In a counterattack with tanks, the Red Army pushed the infantry out of the town. Only in the gullies north of Alexeyevka could the German troops hang on. Hauptsturmführer Becker received an order to force a breakthrough after dive-bomber and heavy artillery preparation. Through the strongly centered fire of the 1st Unit (Stubaf. Steineck) on Alexeyevka, the halted attack of the 1st Battalion (Kraas) of the 2nd SS Armored Grenadier Regiment be resumed.

At 1:25 P.M. the dive-bomber attack began. At the same time, all available heavy weapons were fired. Utilizing the heavy fire of the 1st Unit, the 2nd Company gradually gained ground. But the attack came to a stop again. Into this critical situation Becker pushed forward with a few hastily gathered men. He was able to enlarge the breakthrough point. In the morning hours of March 12, 1943 the Kraas Battalion pushed into Alexeyevka again. From dominating buildings, the enemy put up bitter opposition. After strong fire from the towed-along artillery and foglayers, the battalions again moved against the actual city. An important corner post in the defensive front around Kharkov was broken away. The Sandig Battalion broke through the field positions on the northern edge and took the northern block of the main railway station. What the battle was like for the Lehnert Battery is shown by Horst Mutterlose: "Our grenadiers were held fast at the level of the cemetery. The attack got stuck. The first tall buildings were close at hand. Now we had to help the grenadiers. We wanted to concentrate artillery fire on the street by the buildings and make the break into the city easier. Shots flew from the side and ahead. We could not see through the growth of trees and brush. The Russians fired explosive shells. We fired our shells with exploding points set high, to see just where our shots were falling. We had fired at least three shells with approproate corrections. Although we heard the detonations clearly, we could not see where they hit."

The units of the Leibstandarte SS Adolf Hitler gathered for the decisive push against Kharkov. Light howitzers of the 1st Unit are seen on the march to the north. A thaw has begun.

Above: *Heavy howitzers open the approaches to the city! A gun crew awaits the command to fire. The wind blows cold over the barren landscape. Hooded jackets do their job well.* Below: *An air view of central Kharkov with Red Square in the middle, surrounded by tall buildings in American style.*

"It was too much for our battery chief. He, who used his weapon masterfully, was now to delay the attack at the decisive moment? Although the Russians shells whistled around our SPW, Obersturmführer Lehnert jumped from his vehicle full of desperation. In a few steps he stood beside a hut where he had a better view. Again a command to fire came. "Fired!" I shouted to the Chief. Seconds later the point at which the shell exploded was easy to see, right where we wanted it. Our Battery Chief smiled, and just at that moment he was hit. There he lay, still with a smile on his lips. But he wasn't alive any more, as we could see at once. Crippling horror prevailed around the few of us in the SPW. We were speechless. We thought a lot of our young Chief. For us it was unthinkable that he would no longer be among us."

With a swift attack the weakening enemy was pushed back, trying to hang on in the buildings of the inner city. The Battery Chief of the 1./AR-LSSAH, Eisse de Vries, reported:

"Our battle group (Peiper) attacked Kharkov from the north. We cleared the way to the rows of buildings in the city for the infantry with foglayers and explosive shells. After the breakthrough we reached 'Red Square'. The light howitzers were brought into action at the shortest range. The enemy put up a strong defense, particularly with flat-fire weapons. Under direct fire from our lFH 18 howitzers, blocks of houses were freed of sharpshooters. Toward evening we were visited by Panzermeyer, who rushed up in an open car. Later we paid him a visit and discussed the situation." Peiper made contact with Max Hansen's Battalion at 'Red Square' and formed a small bridgehead along the Staro-Moskovska road. With a few SPW he made contact with the Meyer Battle Group where the road forked towardChuguyev.

Light Field Howitzer 18 (1st Battery, Obersturmführer de Vries) and self-propelled antitank guns (Prinz Company) fight to open an approach route to the inner city. The just-fired howitzer shell can be seen clearly (over the water puddle). At 470 m/sec it flies low toward the enemy.

The 1st Battery Fights in the Streets of Kharkov

Above: *Light howitzers on the front line! Sharpshooters in the vicinity of 'Red Square' were knocked out.* Below: *The gun is fired at the enemy with a horizontal barrel. The spurs could not be driven into the paved streets. All the men pushed against the recoiling howitzer.*

Since the early morning hours of March 13, 1943, the groups of the strengthened regiments fought their way through to the southeast. The opposition was extremely tough. Every single building had to be cleaned out systematically. The Adjutant of the 1st Unit, Untersturmführer Schulz, fell in the street fighting. He was struck directly by a machine-gun burst, and his map case was thoroughly perforated. The Peiper Group enlarged their bridgehead over the Kharkov River. The Russians sat in the buildings with machine guns, antitank guns and roof sharpshooters, fighting with remarkable bravery. Enemy tanks flanked their own troops everywhere, in the streets, from doorways and yards. The bridges over the Kharkov River were under steady enemy artillery fire. The Reconnaissance Unit pushed forward on the Chuguyev road and captured the tractor factory. Rottenführer Gottzmann of the subordinated 3rd Battery described the fighting:

"We were in action with Panzermeyer at the Kharkov-Chuguyev crossroads. The Russias were to be prevented from breaking out of the inner city. My gun (lFH 18) stood pointed at the city. Panzermeyer had set it up like that himself. We were located right next to his command post, which was in a cellar. One could only climb down a long ladder into it. Panzermeyer was seldom there. Sometimes he took my entire gun crew along for street fighting. Then I had to aim, load and fire alone. with only one healthy arm. But I managed. Shells fell around us all the time. Along with Obersturmbannführer Kurt Meyer, I took cover under the gun. Where he was, things were busy. 'Where are the men?' he asked me after the firing. He found a quicker way to fire, but in my scope, 50 meters before us, was a high-tension pole. I said" 'No firing field! The pole!'

"Panzermeyer answered, 'Shoot! It will go by!' I fired a direct hit on the pole and splintered it. He commented: 'See, now you have a field!' The second shell hit exactly on target. Those days and nights of house-to-house fighting in Kharkov, how can I ever forget them?"

On March 14, 1943 the Leibstandarte, as ordered, pushed farther forward and secured block after block. In the afternoon the Grossdeutsche Rundfunk broadcast a special report on all its stations: Kharkov has been retaken.

Almost every building had to be taken by using heavy weapons. Careful—shooters on the roofs! The aiming gunner can hardly feel safe looking over the gun shield (3rd Battery).

Fritz Topeters came to the Leibstandarte as an Obersturmführer from the horse-drawn artillery. After Lehnert's death he took over the 11th Battery. Radiomen Dudda and Schuster are loading an intelligence vehicle.

An aimer uses the panoramic scope of a light howitzer. This soldier is an old "Reichsrottenführer" who knows his way around Russia.

Above: *A burning T-34 tank, hit by the guns of the 1st Unit.* Below: *Shot-up buildings on "Red Square", which was renamed "Leibstandarte Square" after the retaking of Kharkov on March 14, 1943, Here the street fighting went on bitterly.*

Two telehone men of the 1st Battery (Sturmmann Krahn and Schröter) rejoice over their newly-gained Iron Crosses.

The Sword-knot Unterführer of the 11th (heavy howitzer) Bettery: Oberscharführer Paul Wittek (intelligence squad l;eader), Hauptscharführer Lindau (storekeeper sergeant, +), Hauptscharführer Wacker (ammunition squad leader, +), Staff Scharführer Heinz Hammerdörfer ("top sergeant"), Oberscharführer Fröhlich, in Kharkov early in April 1943.

Advance to Belgorod

After strong preparation by fire from the 1st and 3rd Units plus dive-bombers, the units headed north on March 16, 1943. Numerous units, including the "Grossdeutschland" Army Division, were advancing on Belgorod. The concept of a race to Belgorod was talked of. After the Peiper Battle Group in its old structure had far exceeded its attack target for March 18, it was decided to continue the advance. The main Russian line was broken and Belgorod was taken in a surprise attack.

The Peiper Battle Group drove off an armored attack from the northwest toward Belgorod, shooting down several tanks. In all, with the help of the heavy weapons (tanks, assault guns, tank destroyers and light howitzers), 14 Soviet tanks and 16 guns could be destroyed. The Belgorod North safety line had to be strengthened constantly. The Commander of the Artillery Regiment was relieved as town commandant of Kharkov to take over the command of the artillery in the Belgorod area. Here Obersturmführer Horst Bartels' foglaying battery stood out for its excellent firing. At the end of March, the last units of the Division were relieved. Thus weeks of hard fighting came to an end. The LSSAH could then apply all its powers to its refreshment. Because the founding of the new "Hitler Youth" Division from the Leibstandarte was ordered, numerous men were transferred. In particular, experienced troop leaders and subalterns formed the framework of the new division. The whole II. Unit of the Artillery Regiment was transferred to the "HJ". Two commanders and three battery chiefs completed the task, for which every battery had to give up several Unterführer. They were replaced at first not by volunteers, but by Luftwaffe men; Flak gun crews in particular were taken on.

After the Kharkov campaign the Artillery Regiment was restructured, partly because of the many transferred men. From then on a light 1st Unit, armored 2nd Unit and heavy 3rd Unit came into being. Launcher and cannon batteries formed the regiment's units. The reequipping of the II./AR with armored self-propepped guns necessitated the opening of an armored vehicle driving school at Walki. Two batteries were rearmed with 10.5-cm howitzers on Gun Car II (Sd.Kfz. 124), known as "Wespen" (Wasps). One battery received 15-cm heavy howitzers on Gun Car IV (Sd.Kfz. 165), called "Hummeln" (bumblebees).

This Unterscharführer from the Unit Staff I./SS-AR-LSSAH wears four decorations in his buttonhole: Army Service Cross 2nd Class with crossed swords, 1941-42 Eastern Winter Battle Medal, Bulgarian Military Medal for bravery in war, and the Romanian Medal for Loyalty.

Leibstandarte SS Adolf Hitler Div.Gef.St., den 28. 4. 1943
(Truppenteil — Dienststelle)

Beförderungen in der Waffen-SS

Anlagen: (Nur bei Beförderungen zum SS-Ustuf.)

1. Handgeschriebener Lebenslauf;
2. Personalangabebogen;
3. A.- und V.-Schein, falls noch nicht im Besitze einer SS-Nummer;
4. zwei Lichtbilder.

An

Reichsführer - SS

Der SS- Oberführer Walter S t a u d i n g e r akt./R., SS-Nr. 242 652

wird vorgeschlagen zur Beförderung

zum SS- Brigadeführer und Generalmajor akt./R. der Waffen-SS

Geburtsdatum: 24.4.98, Alter: 45 Jahre, Dienststellung: Kdr.Aufst.-Stab/LSSAH seit: 22.4.43

Letzte Beförderung: 21. Juni 1942 RDA.: 21. 6.42

Nach Ernennung zum SS-Führer der Waffen-SS versehene Dienststellungen:

Abteilungs-Kommandeur und Regiments-Kommandeur.

Lehrgänge:

Die Eignung zum vorgeschlagenen Dienstgrad ist nachgewiesen durch: aussergewöhnliche Befähigung beim Aufbau der Artillerie der LSSAH und hervorragende Führerqualitäten im Einsatz der Artillerie.

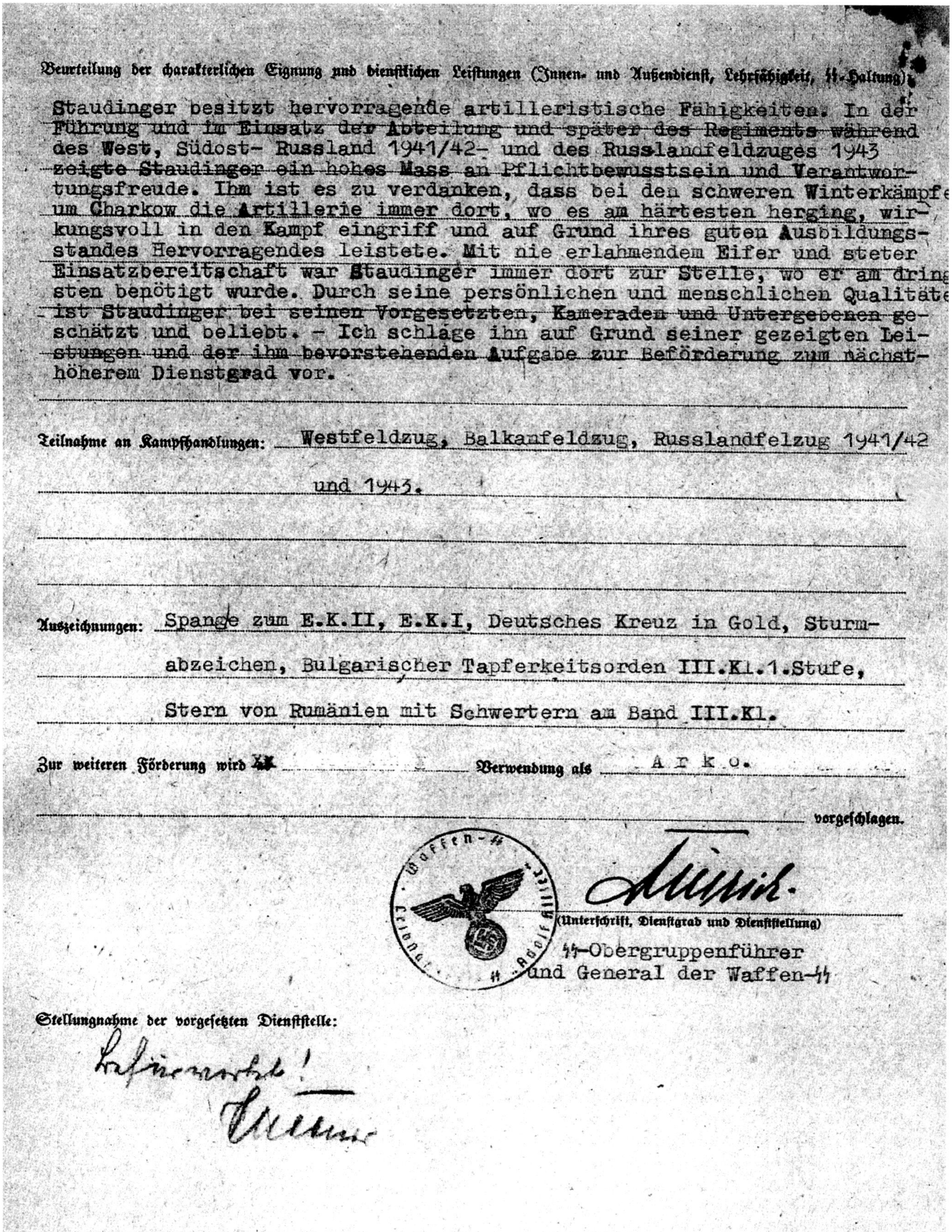

Beurteilung der charakterlichen Eignung und dienstlichen Leistungen (Innen- und Außendienst, Lehrfähigkeit, SS-Haltung):

Staudinger besitzt hervorragende artilleristische Fähigkeiten. In der Führung und im Einsatz der Abteilung und später des Regiments während des West, Südost- Russland 1941/42- und des Russlandfeldzuges 1943 zeigte Staudinger ein hohes Mass an Pflichtbewusstsein und Verantwortungsfreude. Ihm ist es zu verdanken, dass bei den schweren Winterkämpfe um Charkow die Artillerie immer dort, wo es am härtesten herging, wirkungsvoll in den Kampf eingriff und auf Grund ihres guten Ausbildungsstandes Hervorragendes leistete. Mit nie erlahmendem Eifer und steter Einsatzbereitschaft war Staudinger immer dort zur Stelle, wo er am dringsten benötigt wurde. Durch seine persönlichen und menschlichen Qualitäte ist Staudinger bei seinen Vorgesetzten, Kameraden und Untergebenen geschätzt und beliebt. - Ich schlage ihn auf Grund seiner gezeigten Leistungen und der ihm bevorstehenden Aufgabe zur Beförderung zum nächsthöherem Dienstgrad vor.

Teilnahme an Kampfhandlungen: Westfeldzug, Balkanfeldzug, Russlandfelzug 1941/42 und 1943.

Auszeichnungen: Spange zum E.K.II, E.K.I, Deutsches Kreuz in Gold, Sturmabzeichen, Bulgarischer Tapferkeitsorden III.Kl.1.Stufe, Stern von Rumänien mit Schwertern am Band III.Kl.

Zur weiteren Förderung wird SS ______ Verwendung als A r k o. ______ vorgeschlagen.

Waffen-SS Adolf Hitler Leibstandarte

(Unterschrift, Dienstgrad und Dienststellung)
SS-Obergruppenführer
und General der Waffen-SS

Stellungnahme der vorgesetzten Dienststelle:

The outstanding achievements of the LAH Artillery were recognized by the promotion of the Regimental Commander, who became the Commanding General of the new First SS Armored Corps.

4

Operation "Citadel"

In March 1943 the front got stuck in the mud of the spring thaw after the taking of Kharkov and Belgorod. Northwest of Belgorod, the Army Group Center was no longer able to push forward to the height of the left wing of the Army Group South ("GD" and "LAH" Divisions). Thus a Russian advance, about 200 km wide and 120 km deep, developed west of Kursk. The OKH planned an operation to cut off this bend in the front. Strong enemy units were to be smashed, so that no decisive Soviet advance would be possible during the summer. Hitler assumed that it would result in the units released by the shortening of the front forming such a large reserve that the expected invasion of the western Allies, wherever they might come, could be driven back.

Right after the end of the mud season the still-exhausted enemy should be driven out. But the attack date kept being postponed. Hitler wanted to use his new tanks in great numbers, but the industrial production was not yet high enough. Finally, July 5, 1943 was set as the attack date. Meanwhile the enemy had set up a well-developed and deep system of positions and brought in strong operational and tactical reserves. The enemy position map of the Ic of the LSSAH took on more red marks every day.

The Leibstandarte, along with the SS Armored Grenadier Divisions "Das Reich" and "Totenkopf", belonged to the II. SS Armored Corps, under the command of SS Obergruppenführer and General of the Waffen-SS Paul Hausser, which was to lead the main advance from the direction of Belgorod to the north. On June 29m 1943 a discussion took place concerning the movement of the Division out of its previous area. The main point of the orders was the concealing of the marching movements, not only on the night of July 1, 1943, but also the movement into the readiness area on July 4. The 1st Unit marched into the planned action area as early as June 30. Untersturmführer Pulvermüller of the 3rd Battery reported:

"Four the four guns there were built-up positions, everything was well covered and camouflaged. The bunkers for the gun crews were linked with trenches, the paths laid out with corduroy roads. Telephone and radio men had their own bunkers. When I stepped out of my bunker, I could send an alarm over a line by means of rattling empty cartridges. We were set up in the best way. The splendor lasted only a few days. On July 4, 1943 a Russian reconnaissance plane circled over us for a suspiciously long time. I discussed this event with our battery chief at once, and he expressed our concern to the Regiment. That afternoon we moved the firing position to an open field and dug foxholes. When we went forward to the observation post by motorcycle, muzzle flashes flared up on the horizon. Firing noise and shell impacts followed. We jumped off the motorcycle. I landed in a hole that was part of an ammo bunker. After ten minutes it was all over. I learned then that there was nothing left of the first good firing position." On the eve of the attack, the 2nd Battery was directed to a measured and prepared firing position. There were dugouts for the gunners, protected with strong tree trunks. The Battery Officer did not trust this position. He had the feeling that it was already known to the Russians. Thus he sought a protected position for the battery behind a wooded gully. Then the guns moved forward. When the Russians fired on them that evening (10:00-10:30 P.M.), his suspicion was confirmed. In the first position there was not one plank left on another. The whole gun crew would have been there if he had strictly followed the order. Nails were found in the gun barrels of the 2nd Battery. It was a good thing that the gun leader had acted according to regulations and made sure the barrels were empty before firing. Hauptsturmführer Eisse de Vries took command of the 1st Unit in May. Before the offensive he, with the Artillery Measurement Troop (AVT), worked out the firing positions for the whole regiment. The action batteries were given the coordinates overnight.

The artillery regiments of "LSSAH" and "Das Reich" were strengthened by a light Army artillery unit. Strong Army foglaying units were also available at the same time.

In order to counteract new enemy batteries through aerial observation, an artillery attack group was formed. It consisted of the cannon batteries of "LSSAH" and "Das Reich" as well as another Army unit. In addition, [p. 131] every artillery regiment also had a heavy battery to call on if the attack group needed it. Before firing began on July 5, 1943, the infantry regiments had to knock out the enemy advance posts. A battery chief accompanied the shock troop of every unit, in order to set up an advanced observation post. At the first light of day the situations of the planned fire were to be checked by radio and, if possible, by phone.

The Batteries at the Kursk Bend Home In

The advanced observers of the Leibstandarte batteries are seen at their work.

Testing the firing plans (Oscha. Rothe above), and a pause for a last smoke on the eve of the attack (Ust. Protze below).

Armored guns in readiness. A "Wespe" of the 5th Battery bears the name of the late Hauptsturmführer Fritz Teufel of the 1st Battery.

Platoon and gun leaders of the heavy "Hummerl" Battery of the LAH enjoy the last peaceful moments before the storm. The captured Russian DT 1929 antitank machine gun gave excellent support in ground action.

Strips of Wires

Horst Mutterlose, Phone Troop Leader in the 7th (heavy hoeitzer) Battery, experienced the fire of the Red Army: "Early in the morning of July 4, 1943 we had already set up out phone lines. With men of my phone troop we had laid a double line between the firing position and the observation post. I no longer remember just why I used Igelit cable for the last lengths of cable to the observation post. With this cable, wrapped in Igelit insulation, we had not had good results at Kharkov. Often the insulation cracked because of the winter cold. When the cable was driven over and stretched, the insulation tore because of insufficient elasticity. Yet I used that kind of cable, and as I saw from looking at the many lines (strips), we were the only troop that used it.

"On orders from our Battery Chief, we had to leave the observation post in the foremost trench at once. Gatherings of men should be avoided, so the Russians would not notice our preparations for the attack.

"In the evening I led the men, about ten phone and radio men, forward. The darkness came on slowly. About 9:00 P.M. we set out. Some men carried radio sets or backpacks with rolls of cable. I went ahead and the men followed in line. It was just 10:30 P.M. when we entered a wide, wooded gorge. It was no longer far to the first trench of the departure positions. We ran along a rut that had been dug out deep in the mud period. Suddenly we were fired on from the Russian side. Artillery and grenade launchers hurled concentrated fire in rapid order. To save ourselves we could only jumpp into the washed-out rut. The earth shook and we bent our heads to the ground. Exploding shells brought down tree limbs, shell fragments whistled over us. The very strong fire lasted only about ten minutes. As suddenly as it had begun, it ended again. Remarkably, nothing had happened to us. Then we continued our march. We were stunned when we passed by a supply of mines. Great numbers of Russian wooden-box mines had been found by our engineers and piled up there. If a direct hit had struck the mines, our rut would have offered no protection. The distance was only a few paces from our hiding place. What extent the firefall had became clear to us where we were. Parts of the rut had been flattened. Anyone who saw the rut early in the morning would not have recognized it. Naturally, all the phone lines, no matter whose, were damaged in many places.

Scarcely had we reached the observation-post bunker when we put our equipment down. All phone men had to search for damage at once. In no time the trench was full of seekers from the artillery, foglayers and infantry guns. Out Igelit cable, which we had often cursed, served us well. Despite the darkness we could easily spot our smooth cable from among the many others. In a fairly short time I reported to my chief that the connection to the firing position was restored. He shook his head skeptically. Then he smiled to think that he had such reliable phone men. Phone men of other units still spent hours in the trenches, and eliminated the damage only shortly before the attack began."

The mighty German firing made the earth shake as of 3:15 A.M. In 50 minutes more shells were fired here than in the whole Polish and French campaigns combined. According to prisoners' statements, the fire was aimed very well. The main strike was aimed at the "Red Hill" (220.5). After renewed concentration of fire by the whole AR-LSSAH and subordinated Army Launcher Regiment 55, the hill was finally taken in a fiive-hour fight for every meter of ground, supported by Tiger tanks and assault guns. In all the firing from 3:15 A.M. on, there were only two burst barrels, two dead and four badly wounded. After the planned fire preparation ended, there was no pause in the artillery fire. The time from then to the start of observed artillery support of the grenadiers had been spanned by planned fire.

Above: *Laying wires with their rolls of cable on backpacks.* Below: *The attack began in the first light of July 5, 1943. Heavy foglayer use accompanied the infantry's advance.*

Above: *The atack of the infantry battalions suffered much under the enemy's flanking artillery fire from the west bank of the Vorskla.* Below: *Fire from Army launcher Regiment 55 in the zone of SS Armored Grenadier Regiment 2 "LSSAH". With ear-splitting noise the rockets hurtled toward the enemy.*

Heavy howitzers of the LSSAH took Soviet positions under fire.

A salvo from a "Wespe" platoon (3 guns). The Armored Artillery Unit accompanied the attack of the LAH Armored Group.

The Armored Grenadier Divisions pushed northward through Bykovka to Jakovlevo. The Artillery Regiment's main task was to attack the enemy antitank troops with blindage and concentrated fire. Horst Mutterlose reported of the first days of the attack:

"We had set up our observation post on a ridge. From there we could see the whole battlefield. To the left we saw the attack paths of the Totenkopf Division. If we looked to the right, we saw the "Das Reich" Division moving forward. Seldom had we had a better observation post that gave us such a vew of our SS Armored Corps' sector. On the slope, scarcely 50 meters before us, the grenadiers had dug in. A hundred meters farther were the Red Ramy men in their narrow foxholes. Their artillery fired steadily on our hill. Luckily it was more of a trickling than a thumping. That was a clear sign that we had more or less beaten them at this place. Only the phone lines were often disturbed. Often we heard: 'Troubleshooters out!' A deeply dug-out system with trenches, bunkers and minefields had to be overcome. The Russians put up a bitter opposition, especially with their strong artillery."

Hauptsturmführer de Vries recalled: "During a commanders' conference at SS Armored Grenadier Regiment 1 (Albert Frey) early in the morning, the Russians made a surprise attack with strong forces. The newly-arrived Tigers threw the Russians back. Strong infantrty forces crept into a wheatfield in front of the unit's observation post. We concentrated fire and shot with ricochets that had a demoralizing effect. The enemy withdrew in flight."

The firing positions of all Leibstandarte batteries were constantly under enemy artillery fire and ceaseless fighter-plane attacks. Thus there were also numerous losses of guns. The cannon battery and a heavy howitzer battery had each lost their fourth battery chief in those days. Leaders and observers in particular were quickly wounded and left gaps. On July 11, 1943 AR-LSSAH and WR 55 supported the attack of the 2nd Armored Grenadier Regiment and the strengthened Reconnaissance Unit on Andreyevka, west of Prokhorovka, with concentrated fire on the enemy artillery positions north of the Pssel. By utilizing a dive-bomber attack, the Sandig Battalion broke into Height 252.5. In almost textbook fashion it took trench after trench in close combat. In this attack the Launcher Battery Chief (10./AR-LSSAH) and his whole crew fell to a direct hit on his SPW. Shortly afterward we were able to take the tank trench and build crossings. The Armored Group moved forward and attacked. Around noon the 1st Armored Grenadier Regiment attacked the woods north of Storoshvoye. The attack was supported chiefly by the light batteries of the 1st Unit. In the afternoon severa tank attacks had to be driven back.

A 15-cm Do-Launcher of the Leibstandarte is ignited electrically. The Battery Chief, Obersturmführer Horst Bartels, fell on July 11, 1943.

Tiger tanks and assault guns prepare to attack toward the north.

Tiger 1311 of Obersturmführer Waldemar Schütz. In the background, assault guns equipped with side aprons have arrived.

Above: *For the first time, the new armored guns of the "Wespe" type are used by the Leibnstandarte. The mobility of the self-propelled guns is a decided advantage.* Below: *Each of the two "Wespe" batteries has six light armored howitzers (10.5 cm caliber).*

Gustav Mertsch, new Commander of the "LSSAH" Artillery Regiment, is seen before the great tank battle. Fritz Schröder (right), who led the Heavy Unit during the Kharkov action, was transferred to the newly-formed "HJ" Division as Commander of AR 12 "HJ".

"Vehicles go one at a time"—a road sign in an artillery-endangered region.

The men of the open-topped "Wespen" drove farther and farther forward past shot-down enemy tanks and vehicles.

The Tank Battle at Prokhorovka

On July 12, 1943, military history was made. On that day the Red Army, with two newly arrived armored corps, attacked the Waffen-SS spearheads. Since the three divisions had arrived almost at the same time, a tank battle of hitherto unknown extent developed. As for details: At 6:00 A.M. fifty tanks attacked the newly-arrived LAH Tank Group on the Prokhorovka-Petrovka line, at 9:15 a further attack on Yamki with forty tanks attacked the LAH Armored Group, while forty T-34 tanks from Petrovka headed for the intersection southeast of Sw. Oktyabriski. The tank attacks took place with heavy artillery support and at high speed. The Leibstandarte was able to destroy 192 tanks by July 13, 1943.The main share was performed by the Tank Unit of Sturmbannführer Martin Gross. The artillery also pitched in and achieved significant success. Karl-Heinz Rothe, Observer of the 4th Battery, recalled: "I was the first to spot the big Russian attack and fight against it. Some Russian infantrymen were sitting on top of the tanks. When we then had to go back from the advanced observation post, we found that our grenadiers were long gone. In long jumps we made it back to the tank trench. Freom there the Wespen fired directly on the attacking Russian tanks. Heinz Kirchhoff then shot down several T-34 tanks, although the Wespe was clearly inferior to the Russian tanks. He also hit one tank with a hollow charge in close combat."

Rothe's Battery Chief Helmut Henssler added: "As the night fell on July 11, we had stopped for supplies on an open areas of a hillside. The SPW Battalion took over security. When the Russian tanks rushed at us the next morning, they did not find us unprepared. Whoever saw it all thought it was a Kamikaze attack by the Soviets. The Wespen were amid the Panzer IV tanks and, as a kind of "self-propelled antitank guns", knocked out a row of T-34s, I think there were eight of them, in a direct attack. That was the most dramatic day of the war that I can remember. About 100 tanks lay on the field, shot down. Then our 4th Battery moved to the right railroad line as a mobile antitank force and took over the securing of the flank. Since it was very hot, we had the hatches of our observation tanks open. A grenade-launcher attack followed, and two shell fragments found their way through the right turret hatch. One smashed my good binoculars on my chest, and the other—thank God, the smaller one—grazed my upper arm. That rewarded me with an unwelcome tetanus injection and the Wound Medal in black."

Henssler's third gun had returned to the Battery just a short time before the battle. In the first days of the battle, the Wespe (Gun Leader Franke) drove onto a mine.

Quickly mobile heavy armored artillery on self-propelled mounts tore the first holes in the attacking pack of tanks. Two "Hummeln" of the 6th Battery are firing their 15-cm guns at the approaching T-34s.

Above: *The "Wespen" of the SS Leibstandarte are on their way to the readiness area.* Lower: *All armored batteries of the II. Unit had Type III observation tanks. In the turret hatch of this tank is the Battery Chief of the 4th Battery, with the whole battery troop sitting around him.*

The observation tank of Obersturmführer Helmut Henssler is hurrying toward the Prokhorovka-Belgorod railway line. The cannon is a dummy. Only a welded-on metal barrel suggests a tank gun.

Along with the tanks of the Armored Regiment, the "Wespen" of the SS Leibstandarte moved at the front of the German tank formation and met the mass of the 5th Guard Armored Army under Lieutenant General P. A. Rotmistrov. After heavy fighting (two T-34 kills and two of their own men wounded), this gun crew gathered for a souvenir photo.

With transmission and track damage, the Wespe was stranded in the sector of the II. Battalion of the "Deutschland" Regiment of the "Das Reich" Division. When a tank attack was reported there, the commander ordered that no enemy tank should get by the Wespe. The Franke gun had only four shells left at that time. When the tanks came closer, the Wespe took up the firefight, and within a few minutes two T-34s were burning. In recognition, the commander donated a bottle of champagne. When the storekeeper sergeant supplied the spare parts, the "trip home" could begin. With experience in tank battle and two score rings on its barrel, Frankle's Wespe went back to the 4th Battalion.

About his next tank battle, this one in the LSSAH sector, Helmut Franke reported: "On July 12, 1943 our battery lined up behind the SPW Battalion of the LAH. The Tank Regiment led the way. After dive-bomber attacks the armored group moved on swiftly. The battery stopped to fire only twice. Fire control came by wire from the chief's observation tank, which was up front with the tanks. The attack was delayed at the tank trench. Everything gathered around the few crossings built by the engineers. The Soviets got ready for a counterattack. Wherever one looked it was just tank after tank. Germans and Russians rushed past so close to each other that they couldn't turn their turrets. And we were in the middle of it, still with our small field of traverse.

"'Step on it!' I growled into the driver's microphone—just get away from this ditch. After about 100 meters we stopped. All around us it was still a witch's cauldron, but a little easier to see. And then, about 30 meters in front of us, a T-34 went by at an angle. My aiming gunner already had it in his scope. 'Fire!'—and a smoking wreck of a tank was left behind. An ear-splitting detonation mixed in with our shouts of 'Hurrah!' We were hit on the gun barrel. One gunner dead, another injured, aimer and gun leader thrown out of the open Wespe in a high arc—that was the result. A tank drove in front of us and covered us. The Wespe was driveable and brought other wounded men back to the dressing station. The gun was repaired again. Since we had meanwhile lost a gun leader, I could take over another Wespe right away. Only gradually could the battery be gathered at the tank trench."

How the Battery Chief of the "Hummel" (6th Battery) experienced these remarkable actions is shown in the following portrayal: "Without experience with armored vehicles, I got into the observation tank. Along with Panzer IV and SPW, we were in readiness before a patch of woods. There sat the Russians. When the wild chase began, we went along bravely. At once the armored group was fired on effectively from the woods. My observation tank was hit. Why us? Inside the tank was nothing but smoke and dust. After the motor was restarted, we could take cover in a hollow. The shot had only penetrated the extra armor on the bow and dented the hull inward.

"Early on the morning of July 12 we drove along the road left of the rail line in the direction of Prokhorovka. Beyond the tanks it was 300 meters vrom the tank trench southwest of Oktyabirski to the railway line. Driving farther to the north was not advisable. I got out with a telephone. We ran through the woods with a roll of cable, in hopes that we could see Prokhorovka. But it was no use, for the cable ran out before we could see anything. Then we heard loud tank noise. We hurried back to the observation tank. The infantry fired purple smoke signals. Scarcely had we closed the hatches when the brand new, unpainted Russian tanks came on in packs. Before our driver could make a left turn, two T-34s had passed us. We hurried up to the tank trench. Then we drove as the third tank in the line and headed for our own tanks. The machine-pistol bursts of the Russians sitting on the following tanks could not bother our good Panzer III. The first T-34 before us took a hit and went off to the left, making the road free. The same thing happened to the second tank. I though now we'd be the next, but we got through.

"I told my story at the prison camp in Regensburg. There it turned out that Obersturmbannführer Martin Gross himself had knocked the loading gunner's hand away at the last minute. When he wanted to fire at us, the Commander saw the German cross. After the tank attack was repulsed, we drove across the tank trench again. In the increasing heat our Panzer III spent hours as the observation tank. We couldn't open the hatches, because the terrain was still unsafe. We suffered from thirst. Since there was nothing to drink, we smoked constantly." Thus the report from Heinz Bernhardt.

The light howitzer crew of Rottenführer Karl Gross of the 2nd Battery also had a unique experience that day. Armed only with explosive shells, the gun went right at several T-34 tanks.

Helmut Henssler is seen in his command car right after the tank attack at Prokhorovka. The stress of the day shows clearly in his face. At left is a Belt Sack 34 for belts of ammunition, and to catch the empty cases of the Tank Machine Gun 34.

A Soviet T-34 shot down by the LAH artillery.

Four tanks broke through to the firing positions of the heavy batteries. Horst Mutterlose experienced the short, fateful battle. Since the range was too short for the heavy howitzers and the guns were too heavy and immobile, they could no longer hit. Only after reloading did the tanks turn their turrets and mow down the firing position. Eight dead and many wounded lay there. Untersturmführer Protze lost an eye. Fate had decided against the artillerymen here. (see pictures, pp. 146-147) Because of the Allied landing in Sicily, the highest brass decided to halt the further continuation of Operation "Citadel". The Armored Corps was to make ready for action in Italy. But the battle situation did not allow all the Waffen-SS divisions to be withdrawn. Thus only the Leibstandarte SS Adolf Hitler was loaded up for "Lightning-Bolt" transport as of July 27, 1943. That meant that the transport trains did not stop as usual for supplies to be loaded, but the troops could be supplied only when locomotives were switched. Six transport trains were ready for the Artillery Regiment.

The collapse of Italy and its abandoning the Axis had to be reckoned with. The Leibstandarte gathered at first in the unloading depot in Innsbruck.

A T-34 tank rolls toward the German battle line at top speed. The advanced observer who took the picture must have had strong nerves. Above: Radioman Manke of the 4th Battery uses a Gustav set.

SS Rottenführer Karl Gross, gun leader in the 2nd (lFH) Battery, and his gunners await the enemy, observing the landscape alertly.

Below: *The light howitzer in firing position (indirect fire, with aiming gunner Kurt Frentrup and loader Neumann). It is hot at the Kursk bend! Only a little later the gun barrel will be lowered and the gun dug in. Then the enemy tanks appear!*

Karl Gross reported: "LFH 18 in an open field, barely 100 meters farther is a patch of woods. Two T-34s come out. We have no antitank shells, so we open fire with explosive shells--a kamikaze undertaking! With the first shot, the leading Russian tank loses its track. Our aimer proves to be a master gunner and also shoots away the second tank's tracks. Two more approach and we shoot them down. Only now are we seen. We are lucky to have the sun low behind us and the gun dug in. Otherwise they would have shot us down. The whole thing is repeated. With precise fire on the running gear and tracks, Kurt Frentrup made up for the lack of hollow charges. We had just one leg would from the gun of an attacking IL-2." Score: Six enemy tanks were put out of action by the cool and capable action of the light howitzer crew. Strangely, no one from the gun was decorated. The scores were credited to the LAH Flak. But only hours later, after the artillerymen had left the battlefield, dud Ullerich's Flak set fire to the abandoned tanks. In the photo, Sturmmann Frentrup is shown in one of the rusty T-34s. The tank crews were driven off by a hail of explosive shells.

Russian Stalin Organs and artillery fire on the observation post of the Henssler Battery. The Chief watches his men, hoping they won't take a direct hit.

Advanced observer Rothe sustained a head wound and dropped out of the fire-control process.

Structure and Composition of a Motorized Artillery Battery

The battery is composed of:
Battery troop (B-Trupp)
Intelligence squad
Gun squad
Ammunition squad
Supply train

Battery troop:	Observation officer (B-Offizier), aiming field officers I/II, shear-scope NCO, intelligence squad leader, calculation troop leader, radio troop I, radio troop II with the advanced observer (VB)
	Intelligence squad: two light phone troops, three canister radio troops, radio troop III with the gun squad
	Gun squad: Battery officer, platoon leader I/II, guns and tractors, gun leaders, cannoneers, light machine-gun troop
Ammunition squad:	Trucks, ammunition gunners
Supply train:	Staff leader ("Spiess"), field kitchen, fuel trucks (tank trucks), supply trucks, medical NCO, provision truck, baggage truck, weaponsmith, etc., repair troop, storekeeper sergeant
	The battery also had several motorcycle couriers who maintained communication with the individual parts.
	The battery chief or battery leader was not bound to one place.
	In action, the battery in position was composed of the observation post (B-Stelle), calculating post, firing position and limber position.
Observation post:	Battery leader, B-officer, S-NCO, RI, intelligence squad leader, radio troop I, telephone position: "B-Stelle"
Calculating post:	Calculation troop leader, calculator, telephone position: "Rechenstelle"
Advanced observation post:	Observer, radio troop II. The advanced observer (VB) is the most important man!
Firing position: Command post:	Battery officer, RII, radio troop III, ammunition leader, telephone position: "Battery"
	Guns: Platoon and gun leaders, cannoneers, medics, battery locksmith
	MG position: Light machine gun crew
Limber position:	Towing tractors (Zkw.) for the guns, ammunition squad, supply train
	The commander at this position was the staff squad leader ("Spiess"). He took care of communication with the firing position and security.
	The VB was with the most advanced infantrymen, farthest into the enemy's territory. He directed and led the fire of the battery. Its firing activity rose and fell with him if no direct view was possible from the main observation post.

Transport to Italy - Disarming the Italian Army

Above: *Early in August 1943 the cannon battery arrived at the depot in Innsbruck. Since the transport trains did not stop for provisions, Rottenführer Hindel eats a meal on the railroad car. On the next track is a Tiger tank.* Below: *A "Wespe" of the II. (armored) Unit has been loaded onto a car of the "Stuttgart" type.*

A Wespe battery rests in the Innsbruck area. The gun belongs to the 4th Battery (Henssler), which had proved itself as a "tank destroyer" in previous action. Two score rings can be seen.

A short pause in the march at Alexandria. This heavy tractor plunged into a gully in a partisan attack. Rottrenführer Ewald waits by a Fiat to resume the march. After marching over the Brenner Pass, the Division secured connections to Verona. Disarming actions were carried out.

The "Hummels" of the Leibstandarte are reloaded in Innsbruck for transport to Italy.

The children are very interested in the massive self-propelled guns with a gross weight of 26 tons.

In the armored unit, Panzer III tanks were used as observation tanks (fighting weight: 23 tons).

Battery Chief Helmut Henssler instructs the men during disarming action in northern Italy.
The only noteworthy resistance was that of the officer School in Parma (9/9/1943). One light howitzer shell fired by the 1st Battery directly at the command building was sufficient. When the smoke cleared, the resistance had disappeared.

Fighting Partisans in Istria

Strong partisan bands had hidden in the impenetrable mountains. Joined by Italian soldiers, they grew to considerable size and strength. Large quantities of weapons and ammunition were taken from the army, including guns and armored scout cars. To fight them, a strengthened regimental battle group was formed, made of the SS Armored Grenadier Regiment 1, a tank destroyer company, and the 1st Unit of the Artillery Regiment. First it was a matter of encircling the bands, attacking them concentrically, and then combing through the whole area beyond the roads on foot. The partisans generally opposed them with weak forces and prevented quick attacks with strong road barricades. The whole area from the peninsula near Pola to the north around Laibach was heavily occupied by enemies. Tito's partisans alarmed the next village by ringing the church bells. The soldiers of the Leibstandarte were fired on from ambush at bends in the road and places with poor visibility. The car of Battery Chief Guss (2nd Battery) ended up in the Save river. Rottenführer Malina fell to the single shot of a partisan. The action lasted until the end of October. Sometimes the light howitzers were used for direct fire and bands were fired on ocer ravines. The total strength of the bands in Istria was estimated at nearly 15,000 men.

Hauptscharführer Wilhelm Auge

Karl-Heinz Rothke stands by his Steyr 1500A/01 in Reggio-Emilia, The disarming actions ended around 9/20/1943. The Leibstandarte was sent via Udine and Görtz to the Croatian border area.

At this time Hauptscharführer Wilhelm Auge also returned to the 1st Battery. After a hospital stay in Austria, he was listed as "homeland garrison duty-capable" and was to join the replacement troops in Prague. These marching orders annoyed him. Since September 1, 1939 he had been constantly on front duty, and he had no desire to work at a garrison. How long ago it was when he had joined the SS-available troops in January 1935 and done his duty as a telephone troop leader in the newly-formed Intelligence Sturmbann at Berlin-Adlershof. Thus he had one thought in mind: "What is the best way to get back to my battery?" On the night of September 21n 1943 he lay awake, thinking. He had made up his mind not to report to the artillery school in Prague, as ordered. The night did not pass easily for him, as he had just received the news of the birth of his second child, daughter Elke. There was a possibility of bringing his wife and children to Prague.

On the next day he set out very early on the way to Innsbruck. He had learned that the troops were in action in the Italian-Yugoslavian border area. He spent the day in Insbruck and the night in the railway station restaurant. When he left the station on the morning of September 22, 1943, a Leibstandarte vehicle drove onto the station square. He hurried to the car and was greeted by the administrative leader of the 1st Unit of the Artillery Regiment, practically his superior officer. What a lucky chance that the Obersturmführer had duties to perform in Innsbruck and Auge saw his car. When the field police checkpoint on the Brenner Pass was reached, Wilhelm Auge had to make himself look inconspicuous with the other men in the back seat. The further drive via Milan and Venice was unforgettable. The uniqueness of this trip—who would willingly smuggle himself back to the front?—was used for a private side trip. At the bell tower in Venice and the Piazza San Marco the soldiers spent a wonderful late-summer day.

When Wilhelm Auge reached the 1st Battery on September 25, 1943, the result was an enthusiastic greeting. "Man, where did you come from?" and "We thought you were gone and we'd never see you again" were what he heard. The Battery Chief rejoiced at the return of the "Spiess", and he resumed his old position at once. The role of the Stabsscharführer did not please him particularly; he would much rather have been at the observation post. But service is service!

The news of the return of the "Spiess", spread like wildfire. "Papa Auge", as they all called him, was liked and respected by all. He was an exemplary Hauptscharführer and a model soldier. Who would not remember the tall, rugged man with the powerful voice. He could never say an angry word privately, and he always thought of his men's welfare. For the young soldier the considerably older Hauptscharführer was a sort of father figure. He was one of the few very capable soldiers who stayed with the same unit through the whole war. No battery chief ever let him go and got along without him. His bravery and military achievements, whether as intelligence squad leader, advanced observer or battery officer, were unquestioned. In bad situations, when enemy shells crashed into the observation post of firing position, he alwways kept control and gave support to the men as a fixed post with nerves of steel. Through his versatility, he could be of use in all positions.

Erich Dinter, SS Hauptscharführer by the war's end and Spiess of the 2nd Battery from 1942 on, reported: "In the spring of 1944 he was supposed to work not only as Spiess but also as a battery officer and trainer during the new formation of the battery. That was impossible for him to do. So I went to the 1st Battery as Staff Scharführer, while Wilhelm Auge set up the new gun squad. I still remember well that he was happy to be allowed to give up his post. After the invasion began he served as an advanced observer."

After the battery chief's loss, Wilhelm Auge led the battery as his deputy. Such men were the strength of the troops!

The 1st Battery served with the strengthened Regimental Battle Group (Frey) in the partisan area of Istria. Staff Scharführer Auge is driving an 1100 cc Fiat 508-C Balilla. The Balilla behind his car is the rarer 1500 cc model with folding window and headlights built into the fenders. The sand yellow and brown camouflage paint was typical of Italy.

5

Fourth Eastern Service 1943-44

Inspired by the defensive success at Kursk, the Soviet High Command had mounted an offensive with determination and operational skill. In the second half of 1943 the Red Army captured up to 350 kilometers and pushed the German troops back over the Dniepr. Koniev's Second Ukrainian Front had already formed bridgeheads across the river by mid-October.

On October 20, 1943 the Leibstandarte was informed by the Transport Command of Milan in Salsomaggiore that they were to be transported to the east in the next few days. First the tracked units were to be sent to Munich by rail, while the wheeled vehicles followed overland. There the Division was to be equipped for the winter. Since it was obviously not known just where the LAH was to serve, loading orders and cancellations flew for the next few days. Now Innsbruck and St. Pölten were foreseen as unloading locales. Then, on account of the catastrophic reports from the eastern front, the LAH was ordered to be transported at once to the Ukraine into the command area of the Army Group South. That meant that the Leibstandarte was to go into immediate service in a fully unsuitable structure in a new combat area, and in the order of the transport trains (first all tracked vehicles, halftracks, distribution battalion, then reconnaissance unit and wheeled vehicles). To make the chaos perfect, the Artillery Regiment followed with the mass of the batteries, as also the intelligence unit in a second squad. These units had already been unloaded in Austria. The 1st Armored Grenadier Regiment, Engineer Battalion and assault guns were available only after mid-November. They were still busy with partisan fighting around Laibach, and were loaded up between November 2 and 7, 1943.

Meanwhile Vatuin's First Ukrainian Front had made a large-scale attack on both sides of Kiev. On November 6, 1943 Kiev fell, as did the important rail junction of Fastov the next day. Thus the LAH was ordered to the hard-hit north wing of Army Group South. The troop now called the 1st SS Armored Division LSSAH was assembled in Biala-Zerkva. As instructed by the SS command on November 22, 1943, numbering was introduced in the Waffen-SS. Through its official renaming as an armored division, the Artillery Regiment was then called SS Armored Artillery Regiment 1 LSSAH.

The XXXXVIII. Armored Corps was prepared for the counterattack west of Kiev. In the middle, at the troop's focal point, the Leibstandarte and 1st Armored Division of the Army were placed. both old divisions at full strength and ready for battle. Their attacks were aimed at the Kiev-Shitomir railway line and made good progress via Brusilov. The driver of an observation tank in the 4th Battery reported on their transfer to a new sector:

Oberscharfu:hrer Erich Dinter as Staff Scharführer of the 2nd Battery. The "Spiess" was recognizable to all by two silver sleeve stripes, so-called "piston rings". The "Adolf Hitler" arm stripe is correctly worn on the left forearm above the "piston rings."

In a low-flying air attack, the C gun of the 2nd Battery was hit in the shield. The panoramic scope and weapons were undamaged.

Repairing and Opel Blitz ammo truck of the 1st Battery. The big M on the doors marks the truck as belonging to the ammunition unit.

"For kilometers we drove through a wasteland of mud. To the right and left of the road there stood stuck vehicles. We pushed our way steadily forward. Often my tank's observation slit had to be cleared, for the mud flew that high. We entered our quarters dead tired. The next morning brought the bad news: a cold snap made the mud freeze between the tracks and road wheels. With blow lamp, straw and gasoline we heated our tank to get it to move. Fortunately the Russians had the same problem. They were just more used to it."

Unterscharführer Karl Gross, 1st Battery, added: "We were relieved by paratroops. Near my observation post a light infantry gun of the paratroops went into position. When they saw us, the gun leader said: 'If you of the LAH are here again, it'll go badly for us.' The NCO was right, for when we moved out that evening, three men of the gun crew were already dead. So once again we were at the focal point."

The Leibstandarte took part in the combat around Radomyschl on the Teterev. All the men who were not used for further combat activity were gathered into an extra marching unit. For reasons of deception, they marched to the southeast via Shitomir while the action was going on to the north. A member of the heavy unit reported: "On December 5, 1943, about 9:00 P.M., the III. Unit set out. We dared not drive in daylight, so the Russians would not notice our undertaking. We had already broken through the enemy lines by morning. Our reconnaissance unit had captured their advance posts. The Russians had built up their position heavily. That cost us a lot of blood, but all their guns were aimed to the south, while we came from the north. Our tank spearhead broke through a burning village, but the houses had not yet been searched. So we received machine-gun fire. We all reached for our weapons. We artillerymen now took over the infantry's task. Our battle group also had 2 cm Flak guns, which we fired. At another opportunity Ratsch-Bum (7.62 cm) guns clobbered us. The heavy howitzers went into position, and at first we fought against the Russian all-purpose guns. Even dug-in tanks turned up. Then we went from one firing position to another. At night, hedgehog formations were formed and we got some rest."

Heinz Bernhardt, Chief of the 10-cm cannon battery that was at the Regiment's disposal, wrote in his diary: "8/12/1943—Driving snow—firing position in Lyachova—30 shots at Radomyschl—fantastic artillery magic!"

At Radomschyl the Battery Chief of the 1./Armored Regiment 1, Obersturmführer Erwin Rademacher, was wounded and had to be hospitalized. Since the 1st Battery had had only one leader (Chief) in the battery, Hauptscharführer Auge temporarily took over command of the battery. The cannon battery hat a rough time on December 12, 1943. The Chief noted: "With the Commander forward—Negrebovka was fired on and taken with difficulty.—Seven tanks at one stroke! Observation post on a hillside; the Russians want to get out of the woods; Stocker's II. (armored) Unit, fought them at close range.—Hunt for Russians. On patrol with SPW. The next day we fought an enemy battery on the east bank of the Teterev."

Rottenführer Busch reported in conclusion: "In Sabolot the noise got on our nerves, expecially the Maxim machine guns, called "Nervenklaü. The batteries of the III. Unit went into position to lead an attack with unheard-of fire preparation and take Krasnoborko. Entire antitank fronts with thirty guns were abandoned. But they sent us their Type IL-2 fighter planes."

The enemy planned to secure the Kiev-Korosten railway line in the Teterev-Irsha river triangle with their attacks and gain room for a larger advance. Therefore the LAH pushed forward along the Radomyschl-Sarudja road. The artillery supported the attack with concentrated fire.

Heinz Bernhardt wrote in his diary: "12/14/1943—heavy night action for the battery—at 6:30 A.M. we took position with the Regiment on schedule. A tank attack moved northward to blow up bridges. Observation post at the edne of the woods—school shooting (several concentrations of fire)!—The undertaking succeeds.—Fire on living targets—launchers are effective." Above all, it was the Do-launchers that fired their rockets into the air from all parts of the village, with visible vapor trails. The batteries fired what the gun barrels could stand. New marching destination: Kotovka! On December 19, 1943 the vehicles were whitewashed. The first snow lay on the ground. In the evening hours, parts of the 1st Armored Grenadier Regiment, after heavy fire preparation by 30 batteries and strong concentrations of foglayers, attacked to liberate the readiness area at the Stedich. The next day the attack went in the direction of Chepovici and Meleni. A member of a heavy howitzer battery reported: "We prepared in the woods. Shortly before dawn the batteries went into position. The village is completely overcrowded. Guns are brought up everywhere, and from 10:00 on they lead the attack with unheard-of fire. Shot for shot, salvo for salvo flies from

On the completely muddy roadways without a firm surface, wheeled vehicles of all kinds got stuck. Tracked vehicled like the artillery tractors brought help.

A Marcedes-Benz Tyle L 1500 AI (Kfz. 69) of the Staff Battery, III. Unit, is temporarily whitewashed and camouflaged. The eight-seat vehicle was also used as a telephone car. Tire chains are on it.

the guns." The Chief of the Cannon Battery noted in his diary on those days: "12/19/1943—ready for the attack in Tchubarovskaya—many troops—it goes well. Gladoss (Chief, 9th Battery) and Korten (1st Battery) fell.—12/20/1943—still in position—Meleni is finished off with launchers.—In action beside the Cannon Battery of the 1st Armored Division of the Army."

In the southern sector of the eastern front at the end of 1943, the two strongest groupings of the two sides faced each other. The 1st Ukrainian Front was supposed to lead the main move to the southwest to win back the lost region around Shitomir. On 12/24/1943 the units of Army General N. F. Vatutin began their great offensive. The XXXVIII. Armored Corps, just transferred into the Shitomir area (1st and 7th Armored Divisions, Leibstandarte SS A. H., 18th Artillery Division) was able to slow the action considerably by concentrated action. The 1st SS Armored Division "LSSAH" served in the Shitomir-Berditchev battle zone as a steel pillar of strength on the front and drove back the heaviest attacks of Rybalkos' 3rd Armored Guard Army.

Oberscharführer Karl-Heinz Rothe is seen in the open turret hatch of his B41 (Panzer III as an observation tank). He was badly wounded on January 7, 1944.

Radioman at work— "Here is Bügeleisen—two-way positions coming!" (Canister radio with equipment case)

Christmas Eve 1943

Ernst Moll, who came to the 8th (heavy howitzer) Battery in August 1943, just eighteen years old, reported on the extraordinary demands on the LAH artillery:

"I was aiming gunner for the first time today. Exactly at noon the field kitchen drove up, and brought mail at the same time. There were two parcels and a lot of fancy goods. The contents were divided, and we did not let the beginning Christmas holiday disturb us when the gun leader was called to the battery officer. There they received various notes with fire commands for a whole row of targets, for which German cities were used as code names: Nuremberg, Dresden, Hamburg, etc.

"That was new for us! Fire commands were always called directly, never before given in writing. That seemed to be such a new arrangement that would not become reality. And here in this position, where it was so quiet, we would scarcely shoot.

"We were still discussing the sense and purpose of this new form when a cry electrified us: Fire command!

"We had not yet reached the gun when the first command was given: Frankfurt. The gun leader gave the applicable shot values, which I feverishly set on the panoramic scope. The loaders were finished before I was and waited for the command: Fire! Meanwhile we heard heavy infantry fire and saw balls of light climbing into the dark sky. The enemy attacked, that was clear to us at once. We had set the spurs at the ends of the gun spars in a small ditch that we had made in the hard earth. Cautiously, we had also set the lifting bars (iron bars, 3 meters long and 8 cm thick) into openings we had made to lengthen the spare, and all the men lay on them. That was to make sure the spurs would hold. Otherwise there was the danger than the gun would push loose backward from the recoil.

"Everything worked as if on the training field. The ordered number of shells were fired and we were finished. The spurs were firmly in the ground, and at the order to pause, we disappeared into our bunker at once. But it wasn't long until a new fire command was given. The intervals became shorter and shorter; the battery officer shouted more and more urgently: 'Where is fire readiness?' We had long since taken off our jackets despite the fine light rain. In the short firing pauses [p. 162] we sat on the empty cartridge cases and had a hearty drink of Steinhäger. Toward midnight the firing increased and there were no more pauses. At many commands—with far distant targets—we fired eightfold charges! A fairly large additional sack of powder was stuck into the cartridge. Uneasily we looked at the gun barrel to see if it would stand the tremendous pressure. The noise at firing was dry and shorter, and a high metallic tone of the vibrating steel hurt our ears. After a few shots the roughly knee-high spur had completely disappeared into the ground. That was normally no problem, as it happened rarely that the gun had to be turned in a position. The barrel could be turned far to both sides. But here we had to cover such a wide field that turning became necessary, In the hard ground it was very laborious to dig the spur loose and pull it out.

Commanders confer after rough action in December 1943. In front of a light armored troop carrier (Sd.Kfz. 250/1) with an MG 34 behind a shield, Heinrich Heimann, Commander of the Assault Gun Unit of "LSSAH" (far right), Ernst Luhmann, Commander of the Armored Artillery Unit (2nd from right), and Hauptsturmführer Eisse de Vries, Commander of the Light Artillery Unit (far left, in coat) have gathered.

"The rate of fire increased more and more during the night, as did the frequency of turning the gun. Loading, at which we took turns, wore down our strength a lot. Since the command to turn the gun came from the aimer, everybody looked tensely at me when I tried to home in on the target. Not a word was said, as we were exhausted. Again and again we were driven by the balls of light and the battery officer's cries for readiness to fire. Sweat ran in streams. With our hands dirtied by the grease of the shells and the bits of powder from the cartridges, we had wiped our faces till we were unrecognizable. Awareness had long since been turned off. All our activities just happened mechanically. The news from the ammunition carriers that our comrade previously wounded by a grenade launcher had died on the way to the hospital no longer penetrated to our brains. A change in firing commands meant a short pause for everybody except the aimer. One saw how the men's muscles relaxed and they sagged a bit. A Sturmmann could hardly hold himself upright with a pick.

"Every change in the firing command was now linked to turning the gun. A feeling of desperation slowly grew in us. Inspired by our desperation, we had the feeling that despite our last service we couldn't do what was required of us. Over and over I had to give the order to turn the gun, until I could no longer say it. The gunners stared at me, tired and worried. I just raised my head to the panoramic scope, and they understood me. The intervals between these silent orders and the reaqction to them became longer and longer. Our faces were twisted.

"One comrade broke under the weight of the heavy iron bars. He was at the end. About 6:00 A.M. came the command to pause. Then a change of position followed." Rottenführer Busch reported on the further combat south of Shitomir:

A direct hit on a towing tractor of the 8th battery left one man dead and several badly wounded.

"On the morning of December 28, 1943 the battle noise had come alarmingly close.

"In the morning twilight there was noise all over. Ahead, right, left, and even behind us! Afain we were surrounded by the enemy. Russian tanks were already on the road. The batteries fired nonstop. The guns had to be turned constantly. 'The Russians are attacking with strong infantry and tanks! Hurry up and fire!' Thus came the orders by phone from the observers to the firing positions. The Russians came closer and closer to the lightly occupied village. The heavy guns fired on the enemy at the shortest range. One tank was hit directly by a heavy howitzer of the 8th Battery. The foglayers fired a salvo at the attacking masses again. About noon we changed our position.

"The first vehicles left the place, then the I. and II. Units. Only our III. Unit was still there with its seven heavy 15-cm guns until the end. We covered the retreat of the division across the Guiva river and waited for the last infantry units. The bulky sFH 18 guns stood in the open against the Russians. Not far from the village a wooden bridge had to be crossed, and it caved in. In no time the long columns came to a stop before the river.

"Russian civilians were rounded up and helped with makeshift repairs. The withdrawal went on from there in an orderly manner.

"When night fell, the heavy howitzers were still in position up front, holding off the Russians with direct fire. But how were the guns to be moved back? Under the roughest conditions they could all be moved over the river. The Russians followed closely. One gun was stuck hopelessly and was to be blown up.

"Then a Panther came up as the rear guard and hauled it out. So the Russians didn't get their hands on anything of ours. Our next target was Kolchos Beresina."

On December 29, 1943 the Leibstandarte stood as a breakwater, in its toughest action to date against a rolling flood. All the units defended themselves splendidly against steady tank and infantry attacks. In all, 59 enemy tanks could be shot down.

"North of Berditchev, at the old sugar factory, the batteries of the I. Unit fought off a hitherto unknown mass attack by the Soviets. Rottenführer Frentrup, gun leader in the 2nd Battery, described the combat by phone: "Thousands came at our positions. Besides regular units, strong partisan bands also took part. At a range of 700-800 meters we opened direct fire. It was the purest target practice. We felt intoxicated. After the heavy, unbroken defensive fighting of the last weeks, one can understand this reaction. The cannoneers felt fulfillment and joy at their success. The last wave of Russians had no rifles, so they picked up the fallen men's weapons." Nobody could have imagined that the Russian regiments would have rushed into the unloading of heavy artillery units."

Wilfrid Ihle, aiming gunner of a neighboring battery, also recalled very precisely:

"We were on the march on a road and were secured by weak infantry forces. Then came the Russian attack on our flank. Thousands of massed Soviets stormed at us. In no time, our guns were ready for fire beside their tractors at the edge of the road. The attack collapsed with horrifying losses in the fire of our light howitzers. We finished the encounter without losses of our own."

The fighting on those days was recognized in the Wehrmacht report of December 31, 1943:

"In the heavy defensive fighting in the Shitomir area, the 1st SS Armored Division "LSSAH" under the command of Oberführer Wisch stood out for their splendid fighting spirit." The fighting in this area continued until January 1944. The Russians struck the Leibstandarte's front almost ceaselessly. The Soviet troops were always supported by tanks and heavy artillery. A regiment-strong attack hit the Reconnaissance Unit on January 2, 1944; it could hold its position only with its last ounce of strength. The Armored Unit (II./Pz.AR 1) took up firing positions with its "Wespen" and "Hummeln", contributing much to the success. The self-propelled guns attacked with horizontal guns and scored much success with their direct fire.

The Red Army almost caught the Artillery Regiment on January 5, 1944. Rottenführer Busch noted: "The regimental command post and batteries were attacked. Every man reached for his gun after Russian tanks and infantry broke into Ratschki. Hauptsturmführer Herbert Fork, Chief of the 7th [p. 164] Battery, gathered the men hastily and made a counterattack. He chased the Russians away over a hill. In Yanushpol the supply train was attacked. In the 2nd Battery the Russians grabbed the provisions. One Russian carried a flour bag on his shoulders. In the counterattack the shots went into the flour bag. So he left a trail of flour behind him. Despite all the excitement, the artillerymen had to laugh at that."

A remarkable thing happend to the cannon battery in those first days of January. "Our eight-ton towing tractor was broken down with a broken rear axle. When it was repaired, we wanted to follow our unit.

"One morning the Russians attacked us. At about 200 meters they came stamping through the snow, 150 to 200 men. The devil knows where they came from. We all ran to our guns. Explosive charges into the guns, vehicles hooked up, everything was done in a few minutes. Our cannons, to which we were so attached, flew into the air. There was no time for feelings; the Russians were there.

"From house to house, covering each other, we dropped back. Then came a stream and an open area sloping slightly upward and ending at a burning house. This area was critical. The Russians practiced target shooting on us. A sergeant of the Wehrmacht who had joined us lost half a cheek and had a hole in his back. We bandaged the man, who left us thankfully. From the cover of the burning house we checked the situation. By chance we found an abandoned 7.5 cm antitank gun with its ammunition. As artillerymen, we acted at once and made a virtue of necessity, We put the gun in positoon and fired exploding shells at the pursuing Russians. Now the situation was reversed and the Russians were on the run. In our excitement and our fury at the loss of our own guns we fired on anything that moved. We few men held this small height against every attack all day. An Unterscharführer of our battery was badly wounded in the leg by an exploding shell. After dark, tracer fire came at us from behind; the Russians had gone around us. Two tanks appeared and rescued us." Thus Rottenführer Hindel's report ended.

On January 4, 1944. 40 tanks with infantrymen sitting on them rolled over their own main battle line between the two SS Armored Grenadier Regiments 1 and 2. They pushed forward to Stepok and Sherepki. At that line they were stopped by the concentrated fire of the Armored Artillery Regiment and completely shattered by a pincer attack of the LSSAH Armored Regiment (Peiper). Single tanks moved up to the artillery's firing positions and were shot down by direct fire. In all, 33 T-34 tanks and seven assault guns were destroyed there. After tank attacks on Krassnopol had been stopped by heavy antitank fire on the previous days, a new advance was attempted on January 17, 1944. Thgis time the observer of the I. Unit led the attack and experienced a remarkable day.

SS Unterscharführer Karl Gross, observer of the 1st Battery, drove off a Soviet infantry attack south of Shitomir in close combat. Armed only with pistols, he and his radiomen fought against the Reds. He was able to knock out the Russian leader with a single shot, and then the attack collapsed. Karl Gross joined the 1st Battery in November 1943 after advanced-observer training, and became the successor to the late Oscha. Hafner. He wore the latter's cap with its single bullet hole until 1945.

Above: *The Leibstandarte's cannon battery is ready for direct fire! The battery officer's command post is protected by a wall of earth.* Below: *A short pause for the 4th Battery of Wespen on January 12, 1944. Sturmmann Walter Koch, sitting on the self-propelled gun, became the driver of the gun of Uscha. Helmut Klockmann (third from left).*

A Rifle on a Panther

SS Unterscharführer Fritz Gottzmann of the 3rd Battery reported on his action as advanced observer in the Leibstandarte's Panther Unit: "That pure tank attacks were often prepared for and supported by artillery was an everyday event. But that an artillery observer rode along on a tank so he could direct the necessary fire support on disturbing targets was extraordinary.

"I was assigned to the tanks at advanced observer for this action to direct the fire of our light 1st Unit with their 10.5-cm lFH 18 guns. The task was a limited attack over 7-9 km, to free an encircled battle group of a neighboring division.

"The Commander of the Panther Unit, Sturmbannführer Kuhlmann, told the artillery leaders: 'It is an attempt,' in their situation discussion. They doubted whether smooth cooperation between tanks and artillery (motorized tractors) would succeed. The chief difficulties were expected in the transmission of information.

"For the last conference w—about ten tank commanders and I—stood in a semicircle around the Commander. 'All clear?'—'Jawohl!' I climbed onto the tank I was assigned to, behind the turret with my legs in the entry hatch, which was in back on the Panther. There was one too many on board, for to be fully ready to fight, the tank had no place for me. Naturally, they couldn't do without a tank commander. My upper body was protected only by the turret, and so I observed the situation and the development of the tank attack.

"The tanks had lined up according to width and depth, and formed a weighty, impressive scene. We moved smoothly toward the Russian lines. Every hill, every dip that we crossed gave me a hearty shaking. We stopped only to give each other support by firing. Front-line Russians ran for their lives, but we were interested only in the antitank guns. Soon we recognized muzzle blasts on the horizon. We stopped and rolled back to take cover. But the defensive fire had already picked us up. The Russian artillery shells fell and exploded between our tanks, splinters whistled past my ears. I tried to get farther and farther into the hatch. Antitank shells fell on our flanks but bounced off our slanted armor to the side or over the turret. All hell broke loose around me.

"Until then I could not be sure what our artillery was doing, since I was simply not finished with zeroing in. Because of the heavy enemy fire, for one thing, but also because of the poor communications. The fire commands did not get through; instead I constantly got questions about misunderstood information. I became very furious. So the intelligence people were right to have doubts.

"Imagine the communication route: My commands to fire were shouted through the hatch to the tank commander because of the battle and engine noise; he passed them on to the radioman. Then they went to the post, which consisted of one tank left at our starting point. They were sent on by radio to our unit's command post (Hauptsturmführer de Vries), to be given by phone to the batteries' firing positions. And where we were, the battle raged on at full strength. Our Panthers fired, rolled on, turned to good firing positions and fired again.

"Finally I also had my target in view. When I could pass on: 'Attention—fire command! Whole unit—fifth round. Impact fuses-from 65 to 68 hundred in 25-meter jumps—Fire away!' A load fell off my mind. It took only a moment until the level fire struck the Russian positions. It had its effect! The opposition was broken and the way was free. My action had paid off!"

Obersturmbannführer Gustav Mertsch (who held the German Cross in gold since 9/2/1943), Commander of the SS Armored Artillery Regiment 1 in the decisive phase from spring 1943 to May 1944. The Commander was feared for his tough leadership. At that time the regiment was fully ready for action in difficult positions and fulfilled the highest demands. His heavy concentrations of fire were well known.

Observer Rothe is Wounded

"During our withdrawal fighting on January 7, 1944. our grenadiers had dug in on a slight rise a few kilometers before T. In the lowlands before our positions was a village. With binoculars we could see the Ivans running around in their snow coats. From time to time they fired their 7.62 cm Ratsch-Bum guns at us.

"In the afternoon I, as advanced observer of our 4th Battery, came to the infantry's position. Not much was wrong, just the Russian guns spitting their deadly loads at us often. My repairmen had to patch the wires constantly, for they often went dead. Damned nonsense—not even barrage fire was used here. Our battle line ran to the right from the road that led to the Russians. I myself was about 50 meters to the right of the road. To my left was a grenadier's foxhole, ten meters beyond was a light two-man machine gun. Then no-man's-land began!

"I was told that there had been a tank battle a few kilometers to the left of our position that morning. But our tanks had come back. Only the advanced observer of the cannon battery was still there with an infantry unit. Where exactly?—Nobody knew!

"About 10:00 P.M. the electric repairmen came back from the battery. They brought coffee and potato fritters. They they had to leave again. I was in a hole to the right of the road. Since it was very quiet, I went to the other side of the road and talked with the grenadiers. It snowed heavily, the wind blew cold toward the east. We joked that the Russians would run into a snowstorm if they attacked. We laughed too soon! A short time later I heard engines running. They sounded like tanks. Could our own tanks be up front? One man thought all of ours had come back a long time ago. And I heard the engine noises becoming louder!

"Then they came—seven T-34s with infantrymen on them, one after another! They stopped close beside us. The hatches opened and the commanders looked out. Then they drove in the direction of our firing positions. At the end came two very heavy Stalin tanks, with rows of infantry marching on either side. They spread out into a row of riflemen, no more than twenty meters from us. After this fright I jumped into my hole for my light machine gun.

A heavy howitzer on Panzer IV chassis ("Hummel") in winter combat at the beginning of 1944.

"My pistol was jammed, the man beside me took a bullet in the back, I was hit on my steel helmet. The bullet slid off, pierced the helmet's rim and went through my right ear. We could thank only our thrown hand grenades for felling the Russians, and letting us come out of the hole. Two of the four of us had fallen. The man with the bullet in his back and I ran in the direction of no-man's-land. When I came out of my hole I was hit again in the hip." Thus reported Karl-Heinz Rothe. Oberscharführer Rothe fought his way through the black of night, the cold and driving snow, in pain and losing blood, back along the cannon battery's phone cable. He could no longer use his left leg, so he crept and pulled himself along the cable until he was finally found by a scouting troop. Rothe was one of the observers who had been longest in service uutil then. After hospital treatment he did not return to the LAH (see sketch).

Of 288 enemy tanks that were shot down by the LSSAH between December 25, 1943 and January 18, 1944, 31 were hit by the artillery, 40 by assault guns, ten by antitank guns and 184 by tanks (the rest in other ways).

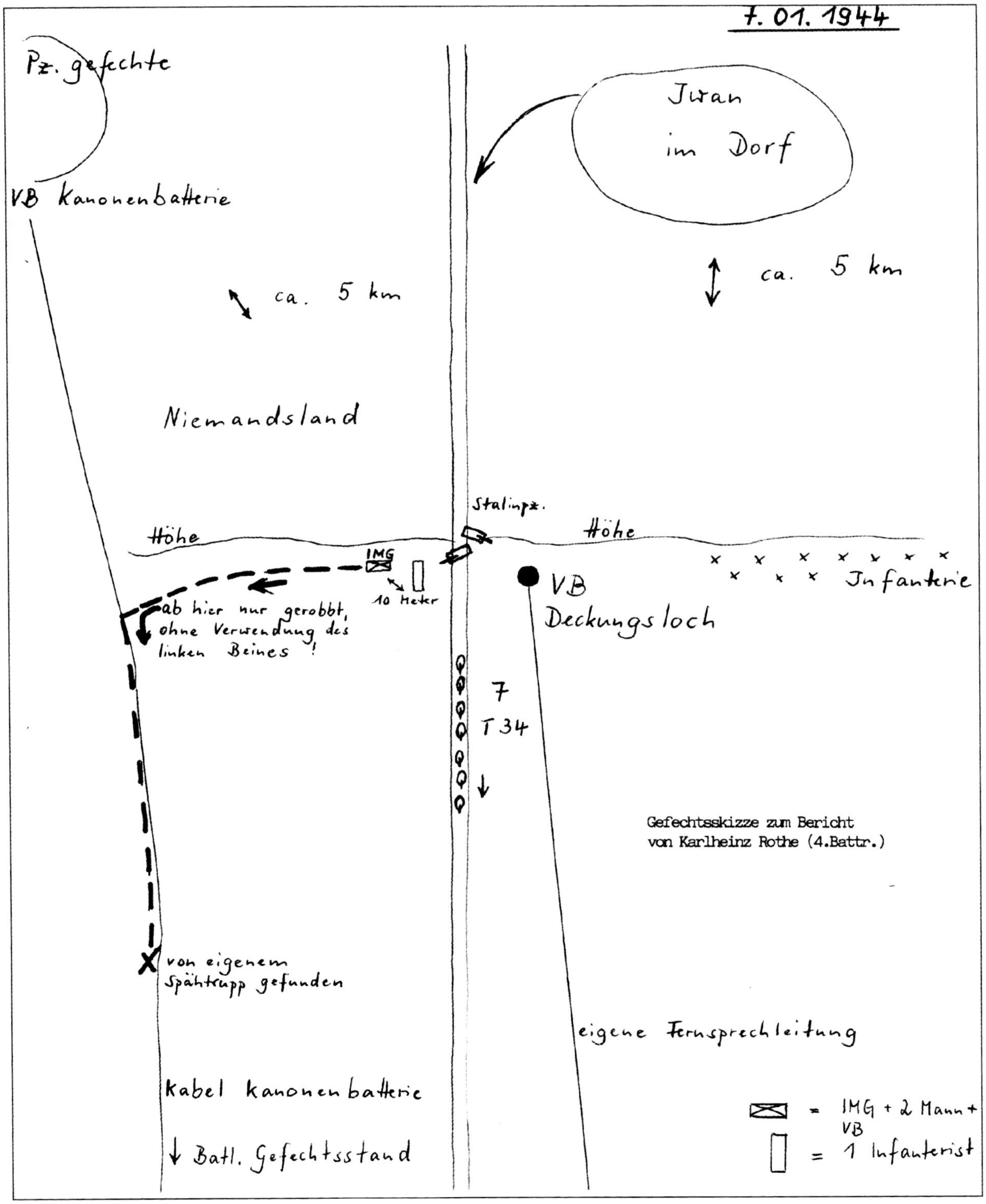

Counterattack East of Vinniza

On January 22, 1944 the Division was told that the I. and III. Units of Armored Artillery Regiment 1 were being subordinated to the 18th Artillery Division to support an infantry attack. The units were to be sent to the large artillery group of the German Wehrmacht in the Turboff area. North of Vinniza the divisions of the XXXXVI. Armored Corps (4th Mountain Division, 254th Infantry Division, 101st Fighter Division, Bäke Tank Group, Leibstandarte) attacked concentrically along the tank road from Priluka Staraya, after the heaviest fire preparation.

The LSSAH followed the infantry divisions' attack. Rottenführer Busch of the III. Unit was with them and reported: "Tank after tank rolled out. A great undertaking had to be starting if one artillery division was not enough and they called for the LAH artillery too. In the night of January 24, 1944 we went into position. The batteries were side by side. The attack moved smoothly. Soon our guns could no longer reach the Russian side. In the night of January 24 we marched out, into a bold undertaking. Our goal was to form a pocket. Our artillery regiment followed right after the leading tanks. The reconnaissance unit came after us, with tanks in between the protect the columns.

The spearhead immediately drew Stalin Organ fire. We stopped in a village. Our 1st Unit went into position and helped the attack move forward. Then our column drove deeper and deeper into the enemy. Everywhere we saw the shot-down and still-smoking wrecked tanks. In the next few days we moved only as a column. There was no time to take firing positions. We had to move fast and stay at the Russians' heels." After the Soviet defensive front was penetrated in several places, it was possible to encircle five divisions of the 17th Guard Rifle Corps south of Lipowez and two divisions of the 21st Rifle Corps farther east on January 28, 1944. These units were able to break out in part at night. But the Russians had to retreat over 30 kilometers there. After the undertaking was finished, the two units returned to the division. The 18th Artillery Division had been formed on October 1, 1943 as a test unit for the forming of artillery focal points. It consisted of three regiments: AR 88, AR 288 and AR 388. Along with three light and three heavy units and an armored unit, the division also had a 17-cm cannon unit and one with 21-cm mortars. 27 batteries with 108 guns, strengthened by two units of the Leibstandarte, provided high firepower in "Operation Vatutin."

The surrounded Soviet units tried to escape encirclement near Gaissin. Some of them were able to break through to their own lines. "Hummeln" drove the escapees back with direct fire (gun at right) or at close range!

Action of the Strengthened 18th Artillery Division

Above: *A Wespe battery fires! Like the armored unit of the Leibstandarte, the 1st Unit of the Artillery Regiment 88 consisted of two "Wespe" and one "Hummel" batteries.* Below: *The 15-cm self-propelled "Hummel" guns look massive and threatening in the snow-covered landscape. With their white paint, they scarcely stand out from the background.*

Attacks and Pocket Battles

After clearing up the situation on the north wing of Army Group South, the Leibstandarte had to enter into another "fireman" action. A Russian advance against the far-advanced Dniepr positions near Kanev encircled parts of the 8th Army. Among them were the 5th SS Armored Division "Viking" and the motorized SS "Wallonien" Brigade under Sturmbannführer Lippert. In all, 50,000 German soldiers were surrounded and needed to break out.

For this purpose the High Command of the Army Group South gathered all available armored units under the III. Armored Corps. They were the 1st, 16th and 17th Armored Divisions, Bäke Armored Group, 198th Infantry Division, and Leibstandarte SS A.H.

On February 2, 1944, as the weather suddenly warmed up, the massive spring mud season, the "Rasputizä, began. The heavy Ukrainian soil had mixed with the slush into a tough mush. All movements got stuck in knee-deep mud. Stuck vehicles froze fast overnight in a light frost. Even tracked vehicles got stuck in the "lavä of mud. Thus the columns crept forward side by side at a snail's pace. All the men had their minds on helping their friends, but they had the worry of not belnig in place at the right time. Thus the units of the divisions arrived in the new battle zone in dribbles. Battle groups were formed with the task of protecting the north flank of the assault group. In the night of February 17, 1944 the encircled troops began to break out. The LSSAH was to reach Oktyabr as soon as possible in order to contact the 1st Armored Division and create the conditions for the union with the escaping units. The 1st Unit was among the leading parts of the division (at Lyssianka with the Heimann Battle Group). The group immediately began to attack Height "239.0". Despite their bravest efforts, it was not possible to take the important "bolt-closing" wooded area between the relief group in Lyssianka and the enclosed front near Chenderovka. But the spearhead was still about nine kilometers from the encircled troops. To break the ring of the 5th Guard Armored Army by themselves from outside was impossible for the insufficient relief group.

Around noon on February 17 the first "Viking" troops reached the positions of SS Armored Grenadier Regiment 1 north of Lyssianka. Eisse de Vries, Commander of the 1st Unit, reported: "After tough defensive fighting, I could greet Herbert Gille, Division Commander of "Viking", and other comrades of the former SS Division "Das Reich" at the front."

Karl Gross, advanced observer of the 1st Battery, added: "At the opening place of the Cherkassyke pocket you could shed tears. With wet, frozen uniforms, icicles on their coat seams, the men arrived. First they had to swim a river. the Gniloi Tikich, at high water. Many of them drowned. We treated the men with hot tea and clean clothing." Tractors of the Artillery Regiment were used to bring up field kitchens and medical supplies. Even though all the materials were lost, most of the men could be saved.

A few days later Hauptsturmführer Eisse de Vries suffered a severe abdominal injury in a fight against the powers of nature. His adjutant Pulvermüller recalled: "We stood in a column. The Commander was exhausted by the constant action and leaned on the radiator of the car. I was falling asleep. Suddenly the car slid off the mushy road. I cried out: 'Look out!—the car!' but it was too late.

"In the process de Vries was pressed against the vehicle in front with all its projecting corners, angles and brackets. He was stuck between the two vehicles, his abdominal wall damaged. The tireless doctor of the 1st Unit, Hauptsturmführer Dr. Fraundorfer, was able to signal down a supply plane of the Luftwaffe. It landed on, and took off from, a wheatfield. At the field hospital of the LSSAH in Uman, the Commander, already in a coma, was operated on at once. The surgeon, Dr. Schulze, succeeded in an otherwise hopeless operation." Eisse de Vries added: "In Salzburg 44 years later I was able to shake the hand of Dr. Fraundorfer, who saved my life."

In March 1944 the "LSSAH" Division Battle Group saw service in Galicia. There was no complete front. At Manachin supply units had to go through long infantry battles. The "Spiess" of the 2nd Battery, Oberscharführer Erich Dinter, saw action for several days with the "Grätz Battle Group". With men of the bakery company, the provision unit of the Division, and the supply battalion, not only were all attacks driven back, but the Russian advance to the south over the Proskuroff-Tarnopol road was stopped. Many men of the backline services fell in these battles. On March 13, 1944 the Wehrmacht report recorded the achievement of the LSSAH.

Above: *A stuck Ford truck of the 1st Battery gets started. Rottenführer Schrei had his hands full with the captured 3-ton truck.* Below: *Toward Cherkassy—the 1st Battery slogs forward on the deep mud of the roads. Storekeeper Richard Schrei (in coat, 3rd from left) had to make repairs constantly.*

Kurt Frentrupp with his gun crew near Manachin in March 1944. The light howitzer runs on spoked wooden wheels instead of aluminum rims.

Various battle groups saw service in the Hube pocket. Individual guns of the Artillery Regiment were accompanied by self-propelled Flak guns. With their rapid rate of fire, they were of high value in withdrawal fighting and could have an effect on massed infantry.
A 2-cm Flak 38 on 1-ton tractor (Sd.Kfz. 10/4) drives past a burning Opel Blitz truck. It had shot down two enemy vehicles.

Thanks to the bitter fighting of the 1st SS Armored Division, Vatutin's large-scale attack after Christmas did not succeed as hoped. The great opponent died on April 15 after at attack by Bandera people on February 28, 1944. Only in 1965 was Vatutin posthumously named a "Hero of the Soviet Union" (11,358 lost in the war).

At the end of March, Hube's 1st Armored Army was surrounded by Soviet forces and its connections with the 4th Armored Army were cut. The mass of the armored units, including the divisions that had broken the Cherkassy pocket just before, now had been trapped themselves. In the so-called Hube Pocket, the units of the Leibstandarte were hastily united in a battle group. The supply and transport units were already separated during March 1944 and transported to Belgium. There the Division was later refreshed and set up anew. In the pocket it was a matter of uniting the forces in an attack, Supplying them with the meager ammunition and dividing it properly were of decisive importance. Airdropping supplies was done only at night and was limited almost exclusively to ammunition. The troops fought for days without warm food, replacement or sleep. The troops were included in the ceaseless action. SS Unterscharführer Karl Gross, last Battery Leader of the 1./SS-Armored Artillery Regiment 1, made an inclusive report on the combat in the moving Hube pocket:

"Out of the still usable parts of the 1st, 2nd and 3rd Batteries, an artillery group (action battery) was formed. From the 1st Battery there were 42 men, mainly from the intelligence and gun squads, two NCOs—Karl Gross as observer amd Albert Schmidt as gun leader, plus the Battery Chief, Untersturmführer Alfred Haugner. When the battle began we could still use three light howitzers. Schuppius, the observer of the 2nd Battery, and I laid down fire that even made the T-34 pack turn back. Then the ammunition we had brought along ran out. For the time being it was quite impossible to use fire from the big battery to teach fear to the enemy.

"In the following weeks we went back and forth across the landscape. We marched at night. The battery finally became part of the rear guard. Provisions had to be foraged from the country. Every shot of ammunition had to be approved before it was fired. It was a drama. Only one gun was still fired. The targets were tanks, antitank guns and recognized command posts.

"On one day the 'Spitz" did not come forward. Our channel was only 1000 meters wide. There was tinder on all sides. Up front, the infantry dug in 20 meters from a brook. On the brook was a two-story mill. A Russian shock troop had established itself there and shot at the infantrymen in their holes. The Sturmbannführer of the Battalion said to me: 'Come on, let's knock the mill down!' Moving the gun forward would have taken too long, so Unterscharführer Schmidt fired the shells right in front of my nose. The third shot was a direct hit, and Ivan's friends came flying out the windows. In the Hube Pocket all the intelligence men were lost. When my last radioman was wounded by a shell and his helper gave up the ghost, I called the Panthers on the radio. That was very chancey. Only with standing targets is it dependable. It just took longer till the shot was fired.

"On April 3, 1944 we were at the edge of a town (Losiarez—author's note). There was no longer any infantry ahead of us, just open fields. It was at most 1000 meters to the next town, and thus there was no observation post. I was in a cottage with Alfred Haugner. Suddenly someone shouted from the gun: 'The Ivans are coming!' Haugner said to me: 'Karl, come along!'—So I grabbed my machine gun and followed him closely. Scarcely five meters in front of him a launcher grenade hit. Without making a sound, he lay down and that was that. For me he was the shield that took up the splinters and saved me.

"In this position we fired directly at the Russians. Several men of the old 1st Battery were wounded. Unterscharführer 'Piepel' Borak, one of the 2nd Battery, also fell here. Gun Leader Schmidt, on whom I could always depend, and who could aim the fire 30 meters ahead of me, also was lost. So we slogged on to the Sereth. One night we marched 30 kilometers." Unterscharführer Karl Gross then led the last men in infantry action.

Many Ukrainians volunteered to serve with the German Army. This teacher (right) gave good service in the 2nd Battery with Uscha. Rudi Krause and Sturmmann Gehlhoff. He wore uniforms without emblems of nationality or rank.

The condition of troops and equipment was wretched. A gun leader said: "If we had stayed in the east longer, one really could have mistaken us for Russians on the outside. We wore felt boots, captured quilted jackets and chapkas. And we were unshaven and lousy."

SS Sturmmann Wilfrid Ihle, aimer of a light howitzer, reported on the last artillery resistance of the Leibstandarte's last artilery unit. "Our battle group consisted of two heavy howitzers, one 15-cm launcher, two self-propelled quadruple Flak guns, and our last gun, a light howitzer. One night the Russians surprised us with loud cheers! I ran alone to our light howitzer. Although the spars wre stuck in the slightly frozen ground, I used my last strength to turn the gun around to the direction of the attack. Unterscharführer Armbrust, the gun leader, cried from afar: 'Fire!' I fired this one shell [p. 176] directly into the Russian shock troops 50 meters away; they fell in a shower of splinters. The 15-cm foglayer fired to our right, at the same height and with horizontal barrels, at the approaching enemy. Direct firing with the launcher was dangerous; the shells with their slow velocity flew just above the ground. In order not to endanger our own launcher crew, incomplete charges were used because of the extremely short range. Only the top four barrels were loaded with rockets. The heavy howitzers, standing half a kilometer to our north, had already been overrun by the Russians and knocked out in close combat. Our Flak guns set fire to the village where the Ivans had already established themselves. Later we crossed a bridge in view of the enemy." By the end of the fighting in the Hube Pocket, the batteries were mainly led by NCOs, who could gather only a few men around them.

Near Buczacz a link could be established with the "Frundsberg" Armored Division, which had joined in the counterattack from the west. On April 16, 1944 the groups gathered, and after a long time were properly fed and, in the evening, loaded onto the railroad.

Karl Gross brought the 1st Battery to Belgium to be reformed in the Dessel-Mol-Leopoldburg area. At the station in Mol the returning soldiers were awaited by the 'Spiess', 'Papa Auge'. Karl Gross said: "When we got out of the train, the Staff Scharführer looked for his battery. I stepped up and reported: 'One Unterscharführer and twelve men return from action! May it please the Chief!' The good man could not conceal his tears. Since the end of March alone we had lost over 30 men. I told him then that every one of those men—if he did not have a medal already—had earned at least the Iron Cross II. Many also fulfilled the prerequisites for the Close Combat Medal. But in the confusion of the action, there was nobody there to attest to those close-combat days."

The Artillery Regiment was reorganized for the last time in Belgium. The armored unit now became the 1st Unit (1-3 Batteries with self-propelled guns). The light 2nd Unit, like the heavy 3rd Unit, now consisted of two batteries of six howitzers each. Every light or heavy battery now had six howitzers. Thus important leader and sub-leader positions could be spared. Experienced artillerymen had become rare. Since the batteries had been very much unified, the former 1st Battery was combined with the 3rd Battery (new 5th Battery). Similar things were done with the heavy batteries. The foglayer battery was disbanded and formed the cadre of the newly established SS Launcher Unit 1 LSSAH. The Battery Leader, Sepp Landrock, and Franz Kursebauch, fell with it in the summer of 1944. The successor, Ust. Peckelsen, was formerly with the 1st Battery.

After serving in the wandering "Hube Pocket", the survivors of the 9th Battery with Unterscharführer Alfred Kandale (lying in front), are seen heading westward in a freight car.

IM NAMEN DES FÜHRERS
UND OBERSTEN BEFEHLSHABERS
DER WEHRMACHT
VERLEIHE ICH
DEM

SS-Hauptscharführer

Wilhelm Auge,

1./SS-Panz.Art.Rgt.1 "LSSAH"

DAS

EISERNE KREUZ
1. KLASSE

Div.Gef.St., den 5. Mai 1944

Der Kommandeur der 1.SS-Panzer-Division "LSSAH"

(Dienstgrad und Dienststellung)
SS-Brigadeführer und
Generalmajor der Waffen-SS

Hauptscharführer Auge (left) and Unterscharführer Gross (right) were for a time battery leaders in the 1./SS Armored Artillery Regiment 1. They received their long-overdue Iron Cross I with Division Commander Wisch on May 5, 1944, in a woodland glade, from Commanding General Dietrich of the I. SS Armored Corps. Upper right: *Wilhelm Auge's certificate for the Iron Cross First Class.*

Sturmbannführer Leopold "Poldi" Sedlaczek, unabashed Commander of the III. Unit, with his battery chiefs in Belgium: Hans Bernhard (7th Battery, 2nd from left), Herbert Fork (8th Battery, 5th from left), Heinz Bernhardt (Cannon Battery, 7th from left), Paul Friedrich Engel (9th Battery, right).

Above: *After their return from Russia, they march on the market place of Mol, Belgium, in May 1944. Regimental Commander Mertsch reviews the Honor Company.* Below: *Untersturmführer Heinz Hempel, Observation Officer of the 7th (heavy howitzer) Battery, receives the Iron Cross First Class from Mertsch, The Commander's medals on the left side of his uniform indicate his service in Crimea.*

Above: *The men of the Cannon Battery who served in the east receive the Iron Cross II.* Below: *Oscha. Prikryl, Staff, 1st Unit,, after the ceremony. In a special award the Commanding General of the 1st SS Armored Corps (Dietrich) awarded the Iron Cross I personally to especially deserving men.*

Above: *Training replacement men with the light howitzer. Mobility and range had been much improved by lighter mounts (on the lFH 18/40), muzzle brakes (photo) and greater propellant charges. But the gun had to use spoked wooden wheels, originally intended for horsedrawn units (summer 1944).*
Below: *Intensified artillery training with the Heavy Field Cannon 18 (sFK 18) at the Bebeschau troop training camp.*

Structure of SS Armored Artillery Regiment 1 "LSSAH" after June 1944

Every battery except the cannon battery, as a regimental unit, had six guns. After eliminating the launchers, 46 guns were ready for action.

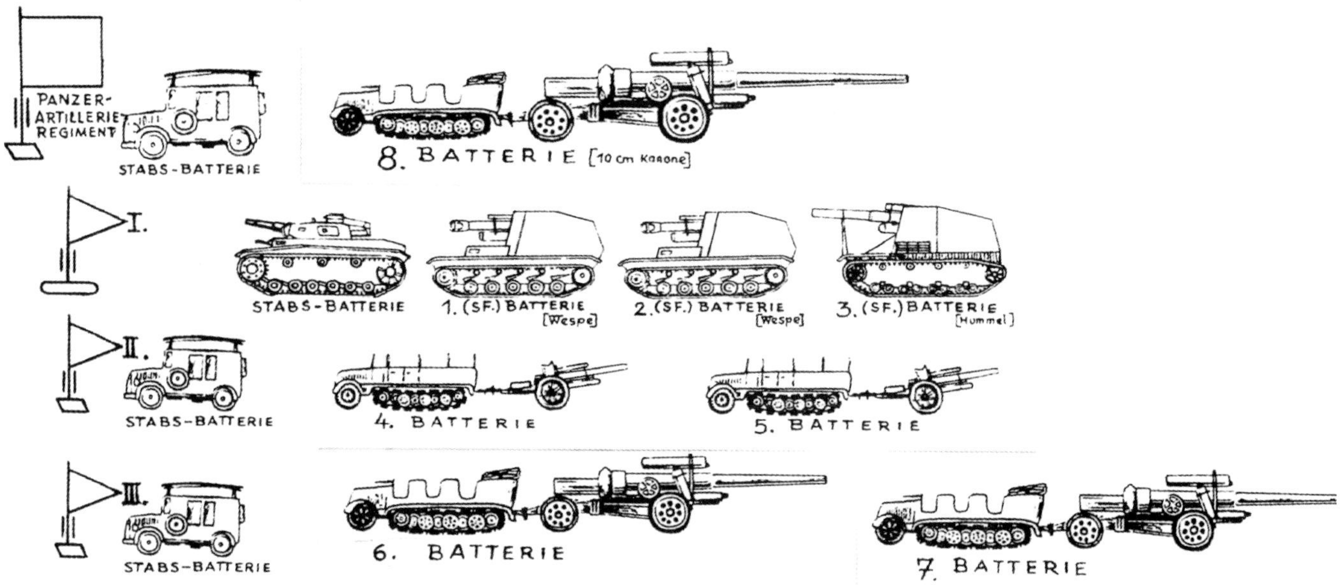

After being released from the hospital, Oscha. Rothe, ex-4th Battery, shared his artilleristic knowledge by teaching the replacement troop unit at Seltschan (Czech Republic). Rothe was one of the most experienced artillery observers. He wears the Crimea emblem on his upper left sleeve.

6

Western Front 1944-45

Invasion

On June 6, 1944 the decisive phase of the war began with the Allied landing in Normandy between the mouth of the Orne and northwest of that of the Vire. The British-Canadian and American invasion troops were transported by over 6000 ships and supported by artillery. The Germans expected the invasion, to be sure, but little was known as to time and place. The High Command reckoned on early August, with a second landing on the channel coast. The enemy's deceptive tactics caused the LSSAH to be transferred to the area east of the Schelde estuary on the night of June 9, 1944.

There they stood with nothing to do until, on June 17, 1944 their loading began. Ceaseless Allied air attacks were meant to destroy the railroad system. Since the Division's unloading area was attacked by fighter-bombers, they had to move northeast. From there the units had to march at night, avoiding main roads, into their first gathering place near Evreux. The constant air attacks on their transports caused considerable losses. In Bruyeres west of Rheims, the II. Unit lost five dead and twelve wounded. The whole transport movements lasted until about July 6, 1944. At that time parts of the Artillery Regiment were still being restructured in the Turnhout area of Belgium, including the heavy batteries and most of the foglayers. The arrival of the LAH disturbed the Allies. In a British armored division's report it was said: "The ghost of the 1st SS Armored Division 'LSSAH' reappeared today. To be sure, in a more tangible form."

The Leibstandarte saw action in the fighting around Caen. On the very first day, the 10-cm cannons of Obersturmführer Heinz Bernhardt fired on the Allied landing craft at the mouth of the Orne. Thanks to their great range of almost 20 kilometers, they, along with the 17-cm cannons of the corps artillery (see Appendix), could disturb the enemy much. Artillery pilots attested to hits by the LAH cannon battery on an American cruiser. Despite furious attacks, enemy fighter-bombers sent at once could do no damage to the German batteries. The cannons, placed far back, could not be located. Even the light howitzer batteries of the II. Unit at first played cat and mouse with the Allies. The range of the light howitzers was raised to 12.5 kilometers, but their firing positions were thought to be much nearer. Thus it went on for several days, but then the other side figured out what was going on. At Fleury-sur-Orne, 3 kilometers south of Caen, the 4th Battery and their light guns had their first action in Normandy. Not far from there was the Carpiquet airfield, around which heavy fighting was to rage later. The observation post of the 4th Battery was located safely in a rocky massif on the steep bank of the Orne. Through a small gap in the rock, all enemy movements could be observed clearly. In their first fire the battery fired some 200 shells. All the artillerymen agreed that ammunition use was high in the first phases of the battle. There was no trace of lightness. The enemy attacking forces were considerably decimated.

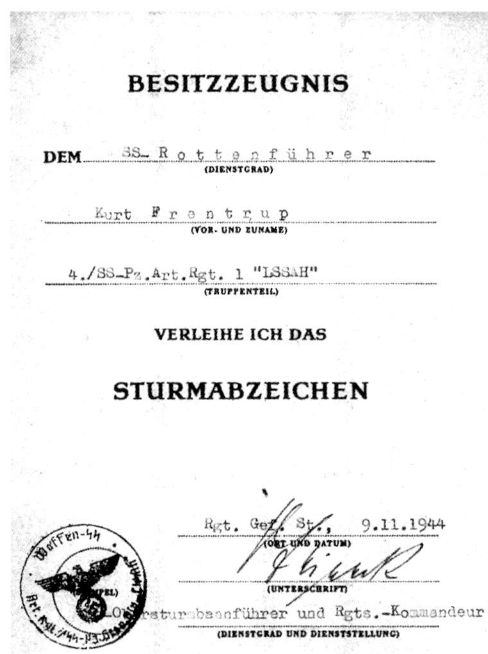
BESITZZEUGNIS

DEM SS-Rottenführer
(DIENSTGRAD)

Kurt Frentrup
(VOR- UND ZUNAME)

4./SS-Pz.Art.Rgt. 1 "LSSAH"
(TRUPPENTEIL)

VERLEIHE ICH DAS

STURMABZEICHEN

Rgt. Gef. St., 9.11.1944
(ORT UND DATUM)

(UNTERSCHRIFT)

Obersturmbannführer und Rgts.-Kommandeur
(DIENSTGRAD UND DIENSTSTELLUNG)

For his service as advanced observer during the invasion, Kurt Frentrup received only the General Assault Medal.

Above: *Ceaseless air attacks on the western front called for the keenest attention by the men at the Flak guns, as here in the Cannon Battery. Weaponmaster Libau observes with binoculars.* Below: *The "Hummel" Battery was transported by rail to the invasion front from June 18, 1944 on. The armored guns were loaded onto four-axle flatcars (50-ton load limit) and lashed down.*

On July 30, 1944 the 4th Battery fired on targest in the area southeast of Caen. Observer Frentrup intensely studies the map with a watchmaker's magnifying glass.

Superb camouflage for the advanced observation posts was needed to survive. The radio antennas in particular could be spotted easily by the enemy.

Despite tough resistance, Caen was lost on July 9, 1944. In the especially hard fighting that began then in the area south of Caen, the Commander of the SS Armored Artillery Regiment 1 "LSSAH", [p. 185] Obersturmbannführer Franz Steineck, stood out for his personal fire control from observation posts. The Leibstandarte's artillery provided effective fire support for the bravely fighting infantry. In the Bras-Houbert-Folie-Soliers area in particular, strong armored forces were chattered in their assembly areas.

Through the fire of a single battery, the 5th (lFH) Battery, a Canadian infantry battalion was wiped out. Wilfrid Ihle, an aiming gunner in this battery, made a vivid report: "The Canadians were dug in at an open position in front of our lines. By chance, we had large quantities of shells with clockwork ignition at the gun. These shells detonated with delays and had a fearful effect. The enemy suffered the most severe losses from our fire. We learned from the advanced observer that the Canadians sent a negotiator with a white flag. Then they asked for a pause in our fire to remove their many dead and badly wounded men. This was approved by us. After about an hour the fire continued. I am glad that I never again had to experience such a thing. Despite all the toughness, the fight was still characterized by chivalry." Richard Schrei of the Launcher Unit reported on the use of the Do-launchers:

"The Allies were deathly afraid of our launchers with their destructive flat fire. That was why they had their superior air forces coming after us. Every time our rockets were fired at the enemies, our positions were spotted quickly by the resulting smoke. The firing positions had to be changed constantly, which really exhausted the men. Scarcely were we gone than the old positions were plowed up by bombs."

In the Leibstandarte's Hummel battery (3rd Battery), the whole gun squad was eliminated by enemy fire. Eight dead and several wounded were lost. This weakened our firepower temporarily. And from the end of July on, the road network was more and more damaged by fighter-bombers. Supply columns, especially those with ammunition and and fuel, could no longer get through in sufficient numbers because of the ceaseless air attacks. The Allies kept up their firing without a pause. The demoralizing effect of this heavy fire began to set it.

In August 1944 the 4th Battery, under Obersturmführer Werner Queisser, stood out in defending against several tank attacks southeast of Mortain. The battery saw action in the sector of the 2nd SS Armored Division "Das Reich". After the first tank attack had been beaten off, with heavy losses for the Americans, another preparation was made in a light patch of woods. The advanced observer of the 4th Battery took cover behind a wrecked Sherman tank and directed the artillery fire at his own location, to prevent a breakthrough. One radioman was wounded in the arm by a bullet. The Battalion Commander of "Das Reich" shot down two Shermans with an antitank weapon. The country was peppered with burning and immobile enemy tanks. Shortly after the second attack was driven off, the observer suffered a severe chest wound from shell fragments. His deputy (Rasch) fell a few days later, and the radiomen (including Mockenhaupt) were taken prisoner.

In mid-August 1944 the Allied forces formed a pocket near Argentan and Falaise, around the 1st SS Armored Division "Leibstandarte SS Adolf Hitler" and others were enclosed. A certain freedom of action allowed the 2nd SS Armored Division 'Das Reich" to stay outside the pocket and provide relief action.

In the Falaise pocket the Leibstandarte was pushed together into a small space. Despite great losses, they were able to break out toward the east. Many units were wiped out thereby. The 7th Battery under Hauptsturmführer Herbert Fork and the 5th Battery were taken prisoner. Only Wilfrid Ihle and about five men of the 5th Battery could fight their way out. Ihle hung onto a self-propelled gun and was lucky to be on the right side. As they drove through the enemy line, the men on the other side of the armored vehicle were shot down by the enemy. The sister battery also went through a bloodbath. The "Spiess" of the 4th Battery, Oberscharführer Dinter, had to report 36 losses on August 24, 1944. Most of them were taken prisoner.

After the Division Commander, Teddy Wisch, was wounded during the breakthrough from the pocket north of Argentan on August 20, 1944, the Commander of the SS Armored Artillery Regiment 1, Obersturmbannführer Franz Steineck, took command of the 1st SS Armored Division "Leibstandarte".

After the loss of almost all the leaders, it was thanks to his personal action that the scattered survisors of the division could be combined into battle groups again and again. Near Marle, Avesnes and Charleroi the battle groups led by Steineck were able, by using their last gun, to keep the withdrawal route open until the mass of the units had gotten out. Valuable war materials were thus saved, while the enemy suffered heavy losses in men and materials. A new German defensive line was formed on the West Wall. The Leibstandarte had to be completely refreshed in Germany. For this the units were gathered in the Siegburg area as of September 1944. The increased building-up of the reserves took place in their final garrison area near Lübbecke.

Above: *For weeks, heavy fighting raged around Caen. This street in a suburb has been turned to rubble.* Below: *The 15-cm Do-launcher of the Leibstandarte Adolf Hitler fires its shots at the enemy near Caen.*

In the firing position of the heavy SS Corps Artillery, Uscha. Lengner sits in front of a tent (see Appendix).

Beside a light howitzer, shells lie ready to be fired. A cannoneer fills the cartridges with propellant charges. Various numbers of small bags were put in, depending on the required range. The motorized battery carried ammunition in the towing tractors (each carried 24 shells) and in the trucks of the ammo squad (45 shells per truck). Thus 114 rounds for each gun should be available at the start.

SS Brigade Leader Staudinger as Artillery Commander (Arko) of the 1st SS Armored Corps. On November 9, 1944 he was promoted to SS Group Leader and Lieutenant General of the Waffen-SS.. In 1940 he was still Sturmbannführer and Unit Commander, in 1944-45 Harko (High Artillery Commander) of the 6th SS Armored Army

The Commander of SS Armored Artillery Regiment 1 "LSSAH", Obersturmbannführer Franz Steineck, is seen after a conference with Brigade Leader Staudinger (with white lapels). Steineck, then Division Leader of the Leibstandarte, wears a leather coat and honorary dagger. He was awarded the German Cross in gold on December 30, 1944.

The Ardennes Offensive

With the collapse of the German defense against the invasion in France and the withdrawal to the West Wall, it became clear to the high Command that only an offensive with strong forces could win back the initiative in waging the war. On the premise that the troops fighting their way back from France would succeed in stopping the Allied advance at the West Wall, fast divisions could be pulled out and refreshed for a counterattack. The Ardennes were chosen as the operational area. The 6th SS Armored Army, under the command of SS Oberstgruppenführer Sepp Dietrich, was to bear the brunt of the attack. The armored divisions, after they had broken through, were to push forward quickly over the Meuse and on to Antwerp and the Channel coast.

The Leibstandarte gathered around Lübbecke and was supplied with replacement forces and new weapons for the coming action.

At about the end of November 1944 a great conference with the Commander of the Armored Regiment and the LAH armored battle group of the same name, Obersturmbannführer Jochen Peiper. Some twenty Leibstandarte officers, including the Commander of the Artillery Regiment and the Unit Leader of the II. (light) Unit, took part.

During their refreshing in November 1944 in Holsen/Bünde: Oscha. Karl Manneck, Ust. Karlheinz Pulvermüller and Oscha. Rudi Pens of the 4th Battery.

The only underling present was the observer of the 4th Battery (Uscha. Frentrup). "What are you doing here?" an Obersturmführer demanded of him. But he had been ordered to the conference as a representative of the artillery. In this respect Obersturmbannführer Peiper discussed with Frentrup the possibilities of action with the light artillery by using searchlights. Under Peiper's watchful eye, a nightly sharpshooting was carried out with the artillery leaders. The guns fired live ammunition at straw targets. A final report was given to Commander Peiper by Unterscharführer Frentrup.

Sturmbannführer Otto Schlet, Unit Commander of the II./SS Armored Artillery Regiment 1, added: "Just in the last years of the war the NCOs in the Artillery Regiment had a very high value. They occupied not only the customary leadership positions, but also had much responsibility to bear within the unit. Even enlisted men's ranks were responsible for the entire fire control as advanced observers. Naturally I still remember Wilhelm Auge and Kurt Frentrup (our best observer) very well, who were indispensible in their batteries."

For the Ardennes offensive the Leibstandarte was divided into several separately operating battle groups. Along with the Peiper Armored Battle Group, to which the !st Unit of the Artillery Regiment was finally subordinated, there was the "Fast Group Knittel". It consisted of the Reconnaissance Unit, an engineer company, and the 5th Battery as artillery reinforcement. The Hansen (1st Regiment) and Sandig (2nd Regiment) Infantry Groups followed. The advance of Max Hansen's group was supported by the 4th Battery of the II. Unit. Wilfrid Ihle, Rottenführer in the 5th Battery, recalled the atmosphere before the action: "We had everything we needed, new guns, lots of ammunition, drinks, and an unbelievable will to win. The mood was splendid. We, that is, the 5th Battery with their six light howitzers, belonged to the Reconnaissance Unit. We marched at the end of the long column."

In the night of December 13-14, 1944 al the LAH batteries first took their firing positions around Kerschenbach-Baasem, in order to take part in the first burst of fire.

December 16, 1944 dawned with dull, foggy winter weather, with much rain and snow. At 5:35 A.M. the heavy artillery fire started. The battle had begun!

The Peiper Armored Group pushed smoothly through Lanzerath, Honsfeld and Ligneuville to Stavelot. The town was reached in the evening hours of December 17. At first strong enemy forces forced a halt to allow the whole group to spread out. Stavelot and the Ambleve bridge outside it were taken the next morning. Without regard for the firing in the streets, the tanks fought their way to the market place, turned there to the southwest, and took the road out of town toward Trois-Ponts.

Stavelot now became the decisive battlefield. Every single group of following tanks, troop carriers and guns had to fight its way through Stavelot amid the heavy enemy resistance. The time and means to overwhelm this resistance by house-to-house, street-to-street infantry combat were lacking. The guns of the 1st Unit, all on the march with towing tractors insead of self-propelled mounts, fought alone through the needle's-eye of Stavelot. Only about two batteries in all reached the tank group, which reached the La Gleize-Cheneu area. There Obersturmführer Fritz Butschek took command of the artillery. The Hansen Group, supported by effective fire from the 4th Battery, crossed the Amel and Born to the town of Recht. From here the Peiper Group's attack was supported by the guns of the 4th Battery.

Sturmbannführer Gustav Knittel led his heavy group with the 5th Battery behind the Hansen Group. Since there had been no opportunity for him to pass them and move forward, he got permission from the Division to advance on a different road. At Recht Knittel turned to the north and followed Peiper. The Reconnaissance Unit passed through Stavelot around noon on December 18, 1944. Meanwhile other enemy units had gathered in Stavelot, supported by partisans, civilians and some antitank guns. A bomb attack on Stavelot tore the marching Reconnaissance Unit apart, Some companies were not able to follow its forther advance. A King Tiger company of the heavy corps of Tank Unit 501 had likewise lost contact. Two heavy tanks could not get through Stavelot and saw action with the remaining AA forces.

The American artillery began to fire on Stavelot and the roads leading to it from the east. On the evening of December 18, 1944 the 30th US Division began to attack the city. The American 117th Infantry Regiment pushed into Stavelot from the north and northeast. This unit was met by Hauptscharführer Wilhelm Auge, leading the 5th Battery as a deputy. Along with the Armored Scout Company of the Reconnaissance Unit, he tried to push toward Stavelot from the southeast. His report stated: "We broke into Stavelot one night (12/18-19/44). On the market place everything was deathly still. The moon lit up the area strangely. On the other (north) side were the Americans. From a side street behind us, a Puma armored scout car came to strengthen us. Then the fun began. My machine pistol, which I fired at the corner where the Americans were, suddenly jammed. Something came flying from there, and I took cover. Then we stayed on the market place and fired around. Then the Puma turned into the place. Scarcely had the armored scout car reached the market place than the Amis fired. There was a big noise and the vehicle stopped. The motor had been shot through by an antitank gun. We ran back to the vehicle. The driver had been wounded. I pulled him out of the Puma, took him on my back and carried him to the dressing station. When I looked at my coat, I saw a bullet hole in my collar. We got no farther forward and had to retreat the next morning. Then we fired on the Amis from our gun position."

Ardennes offensive, 1944-45—The battery troop of the 4th Battery with observation officer Karl Manneck.

Stavelot was badly damaged by tank, artillery and infantry fire.

The Amis were able to blow up part of the Ambleve bridge before Stavelot. The rest of the Reconnaissance Unit was thus cut off from the mass of the Knittel Fast Group and could [page 192] thus not follow the further advance. They stayed on the south side of the river.

On December 19, 1944 Obersturmbannführer Sandig, with the 2nd SS Armored Grenadier Regiment, arrived outside Stavelot. Sandig's group was shot forward by the III. (heavy) Unit. This unit also had the task of supporting the attack of the 12th People's Grenadier Division with its artillery near the Leibstandarte's right wing. The gun barrels had to be turned constantly. The III. Unit had almost no fuel and had to be refueled in the meantime, like the 4th Battery. A captured gasoline depot near Bullinen provided the needed fuel. Trucks were loaded with all the canisters they could hold. The units were compelled to use this captured fuel. Only the batteries with the Peiper and Knittel Battle Groups had good supplies.

Meanwhile the Peiper Armored Group, supported by the light batteries of the 1st Unit, had advanced to the Stoumont railroad depot. The supply situation had become much worse. Ammunition and fuel were urgently needed before a further advance could be considered. Thus Peiper halted the advance and set up a defensive line. A supply train was stopped on the advance route in Stavelot. Other routes over undamaged bridges were not available. Since Stavelot had great importance for supplying the Peiper Armored Group, Gustav Knittel, who had meanwhile reached La Gleize, was sent back to Stavelot by Obersturmbannführer Peiper. He had the important task of opening up Stavelot from the west. The Reconnaissance Unit was thus between the Americans between Stavelot and Trois-Ponts. Most of them were with Commander Knittel to the north of the Ambleve River, the others, including the 5th Battery, were south of it.

Wilfred Ihle, aiming gunner of the third gun of the 5th Battery, reported on the attempts to help Peiper decisively: "After we couldn't get into Stavelot (12/18-19), we moved directly to the Ambleve shore. During the first days we directed harassing fire at the Amis who threatened our armored group. Then we threw half-filled gasoline cans into the river. The cans floated on the surface and were carried westward downstream. Whether they actually reached Stoumont and the fuel helped out, I cannot say.

"Our guns were then on a slope under a country house, in position to fire northeast. The Ambleve flowed past us. The 5th Battery fired toward Stavelot to hit other enemy troops. Desperate attempts to open Stavelot failed." About 10:00 P.M. on December 19, 1944, we were shattered by the Americans at the stone bridge before Stavelot. In the La Gleize area, American artillery of all calibers fired on the Armored Group. The observation of an American armored group (Lovelady) moving forward toward Trois-Ponts on the ridge to the south and about to turn toward Stavelot was especially alarming. This group consisted of about forty tanks. Rottenführer Wilfrid Ihle of the 5th Battery reported on the fight against the American Lovelady Task Force on the Ambleve: "About two days after we took this position between Stavelot and Trois-Ponts, enemy tanks were reported. Our 18/40 light howitzers were still pointed northeast while the tanks were coming from the northwest. It was not possible to turn two guns on the slope, so our third gun was pointed at the tank group. The distance to the river was about 200 meters. A small bridge led to the other side, which was steeper. At the bridge a 7.5-cm antitank gun was in position. Otherwise our 5th Battery was here alone. On the other side of the river, a road ran near the shore. It was then decided that the antitank gun would fire on the leading tank, while my gun was to hit the last tank. The others could then be caught in between and knocked off.

"Just before the American tanks appeared, the Battery Officer came up with a new gun from the armory up at the country house. This howitzer was quickly put into position. Then four Sherman tanks appeared on the other side of the bridge, which tanks could not cross. I had dug a foxhole next to the light howitzer and was going to jump in right after the first shot. Our light howitzer was well concealed from the front. Then the tank battle began!

"The 7.5 gun at the bridge shot down the first tank. I had my sights on the last of the four Shermans. A hollow antitank shell was in the gun barrel. I had put a sixth load in the cartridge, to attain the highest initial velocity. Then I activated the firing device at my left side. On the new design one no longer had to use the firing cord as on the old lFH 18. Damn it all, the new device didn't work (technical defect)! I aimed again, changed the cartridge and fired again. Again it didn't work. Meanwhile the camouflage had fallen down and my gun leader Armbrust yelled: 'Willibald, get away from there!' At that moment I sprang into the foxhole, and our howitzer was hit between the spars. But our workshop gun farther up had already aimed at the tank and fired at a range of scarcely 500 meters. The first shot was a direct hit and the Sherman was burning!

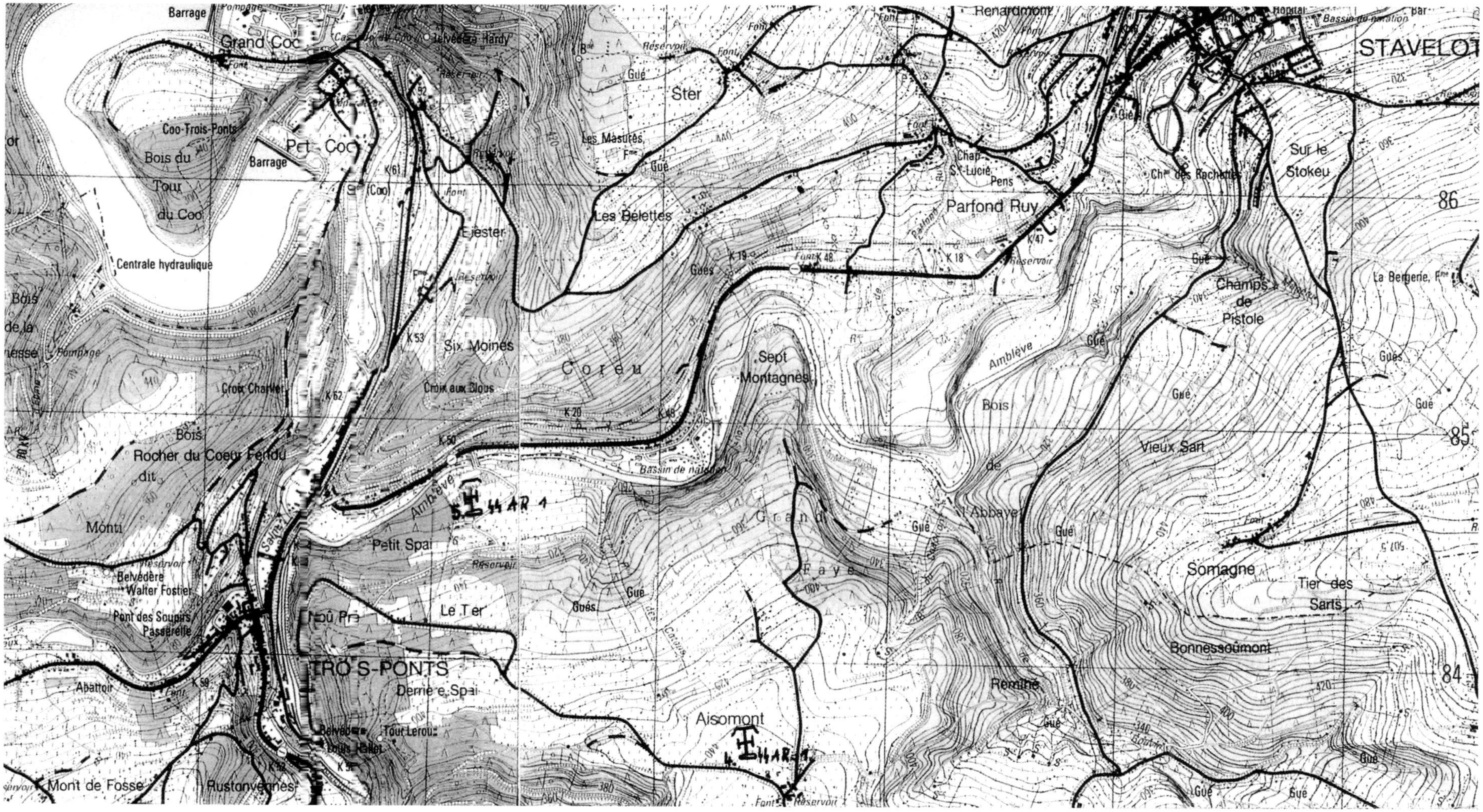

The 5th Battery between Stavelot and Trois-Ponts (12/18-23-1944)—It approached with the Reconnaissance Unit (Knittel), broke through to the market place of Stavelot (Hscha. Auge), turned to the southwest and marched south of the Ambleve, fought in the Ambleve sector, firing position near Petit Spai, tank battles with the American Lovelady Task Force.

"Now things got hot and heavy. Our three towing tractors, that had been parked at the edge of the woods, were hit by the medium tanks and were burning. But our battery was able to hit the last two tanks. The crewmen who got out were taken prisoner. The 7.5-cm antitank gun crew had been wiped out at the beginning of the battle. After shooting down the first tank, it had taken a direct hit.

"When things were quiet, two King Tigers appeared from the same direction and headed farther eastward. The Armbrust gun crew, to which I belonged, then saw action as infantry. Our howitzer was sent to the armory." Another defensive group of the Reconnaissance Unit was able to shoot down six Sherman tanks north of the Ambleve. The 4th Battery, from positions farther southward (Aisomont), opened fire on the Lovelady Task Force. Visible success was apparent. Since all the following attempts to restore contact with the Peiper Armored Group failed, the narrow battle zone around the hill town of La Gleize had to be vacated.

In the night of December 24, 1944 Peiper and some 800 men of his battle group drew back. In a long chain the soldiers slipped through the enemy lines. All of the subordinated 1st Battery reached their own positions safely. After the Peiper Group had withdrawn, the LSSAH was removed from this sector and sent farther south to the important traffic junction of Bastogne. On January 10, 1945 the Army Group, under the impression that an encirclement of the bulge in the front southeast of Bastogne was a threat, began to retake the positions. The Division began by laboriously withdrawing the battle groups at the front.

While the mass of the Division was marching from the gathering area at St. Vith toward the Cologne-Bonn loading area, a few units remained as reserves in case of an attack on the enemy. They could not yet leave the enemy east of Bastogne. The 5th battery was also there and could be withdrawn only as of January 18. The Battery Officer, Hauptscharführer Wilhelm Auge, came through one of his roughest actions on January 13-14, 1945. The gun squad of the 5th Battery, already surrounded by the enemy, had the last heavy weapons facing the enemy, other than infantry guns. Wilhelm Auge reported: "The enemy pressed hard on our gun positions. All their attacks coyld still be driven back by direct fire from our lFH 18. But we were hanging in mid-air. The first shells that fell between the guns left wounded men who had to be cared for at once. The enemy was already behind us. When our ammunition was used up and it was clear that we could not hold off the attackers any longer, we got ready to march out. The guns had to be made unusable. The breech parts had to be taken out and buried in a suitable place. In the night we slipped through the enemy lines. On our march we came upon a road that the Americans were using for strong supply columns. We jumped to the other side. Safely and without losses, we reached our own lines before dawn. There they had already written us off."

Hauptscharführer Wilhelm Auge, one of the longest-serving men of the Waffen-SS. He was the deputy battery chief of the 1st and 5th Batteries.

Sepp Dietrich, as Commanding General of the I. SS Armored Corps, received on August 6, 1944 what was then the highest German military decoration: the Knight's Cross with oak leaves, swords and diamonds (16th awarding). Hitler intended to name him the first People's Marshal if the Ardennes offensive succeeded.

7

The Final Combat on the Eastern Front 1945

At the beginning of December 1944, the first units of the 3rd Ukrainian Front crossed the Danube south of Budapest, advanced to the Plattensee and occupied the land between the Drava and Danube. The German command was then threatened with the loss of the last oilfields. On December 24, 1944 Budapest was completely encircled. Three promising relief attacks could not reach the Hungarian capital. Under the pressure of the Soviet advance toward Berlin and the impending encirclement of Breslau, it was generally presumed, by the Soviets as well, that the 6th SS Armored Army would be used for a counteroffensive in the area of Army Group Center. But Hitler, keeping everything completely secret, planned to move the army to Hungary in order to begin an offensive to clear the area west of the Danube and assure the oilfields in the Drava-Danube angle as a German power source. At the same time, success in this theater of war should stop the Soviet advance toward Berlin by a hoped-for regrouping of the enemy armies.

Within the framework of this planning, the transport of the Leibstandarte to Hungary in the area around Raab began in mid-January 1945. Because of the widely destroyed or only makeshift-repaired railroad lines, the troop transports moved at only Tempo 4. That meant four trains in 24 hours. For the march into Russia in 1941 there had been 78 trains!

The Battery Chief of the 4th Battery (lFH) reported: "For camouflage we removed our sleeve stripes. The Artillery Regiment was now called Construction Staff 15. From our first billet area in Hungary I drove to the positions of an artillery unit to take it over. The regimental commander had never heard of a unit by that name. I was then given the position maps. As I left, the Adjutant said: 'God knows we're glad that the Leibstandarte is coming to us!' That was now the existing camouflage!"

Within the 1st SS Armored Corps the LAH was at first prepared to attack the Gran bridgehead. This bulge in the front, as the

A heavy howitzer battery (III. Unit) took position near Bela to smash the Soviet bridgehead on the Gran.

gathering place for a dreaded attack on Vienna, was a danger and was pushed back in an eight-day operation. A serious command [p. 197] error cut the the Leibstandarte off on a secondary operation. In addition, the laboriously created camouflage was lost. The Soviet command now expected an attack by the whole 6th SS Armored Army from the direction of Stuhlweissenburg. Hitler planned the main advance with the 6th SS Armored Army southward between the Plattensee and the Sarviz Canal.

On March 6, 1945 "Spring's Awakening" began the last German offensive advance. Thawing weather and heavy rain turned the landscape into a wasteland of mud. The unpaved roads could not even be used by tracked vehicles. The artillery could take positions only on roads and in courtyards. The positioning of the attack troops was much delayed. Oberstgruppenführer Sepp Dietrich called the High Command personally to delay the attack date.

But Hitler insisted on keeping to the schedule. The road conditions got worse from hour to hour. To bring at least the infantry into action halfway punctually to begin the attack, the Division Commander had the grenadiers come into their readiness areas on foot.

Wiothout artillery, tank or air support, the infantrymen sprang out of their holes on March 6, 1945. Brigadenführer and Major General of the Waffen-SS Otto Kumm recalled: "The attack began at 4:30 A.M.—out of the readiness area southeast of Polgardi came the 1st SS Armored Division to attack. The ground was very soft and almost undriveable for tanks. The attack scarcely took the enemy by surprise and gained ground only slowly. Scarcely any artillery ammunition was on hand."

The Leibstandarte reached the Sio Canal at Simontornya. Constand air attacks on the spearheads and artillery positions caused losses. Hauptscharführer Wilhelm Auge (5th Battery) reported: "We were located in firing positions northeast of the Plattensee and supported the attack to the south. The light guns stood in a basin, a harvested rice field. They were splendidly camouflaged. I was on a small hill with our air observer, who was to scan the skies constantly. Suddenly a squadron of Russian fighters appeared. We took cover behind bushes.

"The IL-2s flew low over our positions and away. They had not spotted us. But the last plane, a fighter-bomber, came directly at the two of us. There was no time to stop and think. The plane dropped two bombs. I still see them flying directly toward me. There was a noise between us. I flew through the area and landed with my nose in the dirt. It was a good thing the fragments came from behind! My comrade presumably got the whole crap in his face. The other men from the guns came up and brought one of the towing tractors. I noticed that my right arm hurt. The fragment cut the nerve (pratially laming me) and another shortened a finger.

"We were loaded onto the tractor and went off to the dressing station. There was a big crowd there. When I awoke from the narcotic, I found myself back in the anteroom. Still somewhat groggy and detached, I spoke with the medic, who had a cousin with us in the 1st Battery. He was the gun leader Robert Sabitzer, who had fallen in July 1943. Then he made me aware of my missing left leg. I had not noticed it at all. My whole upper body was also covered with bandages." Wilhelm Auge had taken the whole rain of bomb splinters. After more than ten years with the troops, he had seen his last service. Since September 1, 1939 he had been in action constantly.

Soviet counterattacks on the Sio bridgehead were turned back with support from the light unit. After strong forces broke through north of Stuhlweissenburg, there was a danger that the units of the 6th SS Armored Army would be cut off. There was nothing to do but go on the defensive. The Leibstandarte was called out and gathered in the Varpalota area. Here it faced the strongest tank attacks (6th Guard Armored Army).

The Russian tank attacks were supported by constant fighter and fighter-bomber attacks on the German positions and the hinterland near the front. Wilfrid Ihle, 5th Battery, reported:

"Our Battery took a position by a corn mill. We were divided for antitank protection. During a pause, low-flying fighter planes attacked us. They dropped several "beer-bottle bombs" that fell through the thin straw roofs. Two of my gun comrades were badly wounded by them. The older one had tried to run away and took all the splinters in both legs. Hubert Hawlizek from Wiener Neustadt was still looking up and got the bomb fragments in his face. I pressed myself against a wall and was unharmed. A few days later I departed after being wounded."

The broken front had to be brought to a stop with all our strength. The artillery batteries were sometimes sent into very unfavorable positions for the sake of defense against tanks. Above all, the batteries were to stay in position as long as it was at all possible.

Kurt Frentrup , as advanced observer, directed the defensive fire of the II. Unit from the church steeple in Varpalota in March 1945. Russian AA fire hit the steeple, but only the tip broke off.

At the first sign of a collapse the grenadiers also drew back. Thus the gun crews were in danger of being cut off again and again.

This desperate situation, in which the subordinated artillery constantly found itself in a withdrawal, was described by Karlheinz Pulvermüller:

"During the defensive fighting in western Hungary, we were often in a firing position without having infantry in front of us. We went into position and fired at the attacking Russians as they came toward the battery. When we went into such a position, all the land being so flat, we were attacked by German planes. We quickly laid out the identity cloths to protect us from further losses. In all firing positions, as soon as we moved in we safeguarded ourselves in all directions and found the best retreat path."

The defensive fighting went on, hotter and heavier than everThe LAH was taken back to the Reich protection position. It goes south past Ödenburg over the German border. The 4th Battery took up a securing position near Mattersburg (Zemendorf).

As for the unforgettable gravel fight near Mattersburg on the Neusiedler See, the Battery Chief of the 4./SS Armored Artillery Regiment 1 reported:

"The enemy positioned himself at the edge of the woods, ready for a new attack. The Russians finally stormed forth across a meadow. With the radiomen and a few infantrymen, the observer fought off the first attack. Luckily there were enough hand grenades available; they fell between the attackers. There were also assault guns and two machine guns on hand. When the second attack approached, the idea came up of throwing gravel between the Russians. These stones were lying everywhere. When they noticed that stones were being thrown at them, they thought they'd have an easy time. The Russians attacked a third time, this time much more energetically. But lots of hand grenades fell again. The Russian storm attack fell apart with heavy losses. We couldn't stand a fourth time; our ammunition was used up. We packed up quickly, cut the phone cable and took off."

On the night of April 1 the arriving LAH battle groups were pushed into the improvised defenses around Wiener Neustadt and Mattersburg. On the very next day the 6th Guard Armored Army attacked to the north and pushed the mixed bands back toward Neudörfl.

With all their available forces, the Reconnaissance Unit blocked the road between Wiener Neustadt and Felixdorf and brought Russian flank attacks to a stop. The defensive fighting of the subordinated 6th (sFH) Battery was described by its advanced observer, Oberscharführer Alfred Kandale: "From their firing position the Battery had fought off an Infantry attack, supported by T-34 tanks. As the advanced observer, I was up in the church steeple. The cellar was full of women and children who sought protection from the Soviets. The tanks drove all around the church and shot it afire. Along with a battle group of the Reconnaissance Unit, we fought off this attack and drove the Russians out.

"The Commander of the AA (Hstuf. Wawrzinek) thanked me then for the 6th Battery having shot so well. Unfortunately, I lost two good comrades on that day, Unterscharführer Gerhard Schmidt and Rottenführer Seitz." Unfortunately, Wawrzunek and the whole unit staff were lost in the afternoon of the same day, from a direct launcher hit at Steinabrückl.

The further retreat went through the Vienna Woods in the direction of St. Pölten.

The observer of the launcher unit, Rottenführer Benninghoven, noted for April 2, 1945 (Easter Monday): "We saw infantry action at the High Wall." In the last days of April the artillery supported the defensive fighting from positions around Hohenberg, with their observation post on the 1399-meter Reisalpe. All the units were commanded directly by the Division. They all got closer together. A commander told that he had never before seen a division command so close to the troops as in those days. The small war in the hills went on to the beginning of May.

The news of Hitler's death and the fact that the Enns was to be the demarcation line between the Americans and Soviets filtered through. Nobody wanted to be taken prisoner by the Russians!

By May 6, on orders from the 1st SS Armored Corps, all no longer needed heavy weapons were to be removed, while the positions remained occupied by small battle groups for support against the Russians. Alfred Kandale went on to relate: "Our last firing position was in Lilienfeld. I had my observation post with an Army battalion. Early on May 8 there was no more infantry to be seen. They had departed in the night and forgotten us. The radio link was broken. Thus we learned from civilians that the war was over.

"When I got to the firing position, the heavy howitzers were already blown up. Nothing more was to be seen of our proud bunch."

Early in the morning of May 8, 1945 the Division radioed to all units the order to move west of Steyr at once.

The 1st SS Armored Division LSSAH walked the road to imprisonment after five years and eight months. On order, the bands destroyed their weapons and equipment along the way, or took them to the Enns and dumped them in the river. The Leibstandarte's march went via Gresten and Steyer on the Enns. The artillery blew up their guns along the way, to be more mobile and not to burden the roads. Kurt Frentrup smashed his binoculars on the rocks, so as not to give them to the enemy. The Battery Chief of the 4th Battery, Karlheinz Pulvermüller, reported in closing:

"The capitulation order reached us in Furthof on the night of May 8.

"A note on that: At 12:00 noon we must have crossed the demarcation line, the Enns. At the same time it was arranged that the battery was to report to an infantry unit under Otto Dinse. The last unloading was to be secured. Then we traveled for a time along with this unit, and were then released from the group.

SS Brigadenführer and Major General of the Waffen-SS Otto Kumm, last Division Commander of the 1st SS Armored Division "LSSAH" as of February 1945.

At a quarry near Kienberg on the Erlauf we blew up the six light howitzers. All the guns were still fully usable. A Panther rolled into the quarry with the last reserves of fuel. We filled it with shells and cartridges and blew it up as best we could. Nothing of our proud Leibstandarte fell into enemy hands unspoiled. In smaller groups we went westward. The war was over."

The Heavy Corps Artillery Unit 101/501 (SS-Korps-ART.ABT.)

The first commander of the unit established in Soignies near Brussels in November 1943 was the former unit commander in the LSSAH Artillery Regiment, Sturmbannführer Franz Steineck. He led the Corps Artillery Unit with great dedication until June 15, 1944. Then he returned to the SS Armored Artillery Regiment 1 "LSSAH" as its regimental commander. The cadre personnel formed the Artillery Regiment of the Leibstandarte. Every battery sent several men to the new unit, mostly NCOs. The Heavy Corps Artillery 501 was an extension of the LAH artillery. The men were recruited from South Tyrol and were trained in Sterzing.

The 1st Battery was armed with three 21-cm mortars. The 2nd and 3rd Batteries used the long-range 17-cm cannons.

Foresight and thorough knowledge of technology were the unit's first rules. The gun squads could not allow things to be done as was possible with light or even heavy howitzers. For example, setting down the gun in the "Hauruck Process" and, in time of need, fighting off tank attacks by direct fire and then quickly disappearing. Guns of this size were not made for quick action at any place, for a cannon weighed 17.5 tons in firing position and 23.4 tons ready to travel. When a position was taken, the ground below had to be able to hold tons of weight, with baseplates cranked down and weighty chassis cranked up. Just to move a 21-cm mortar shell with a weight of 113 kilograms up to the breech for firing normally required four cannoneers with a special loading device. The barrel had to cranked into firing position previously.

The heavy Corps Artillery Unit was a splendidly equipped group on June 6, 1944, the day of the invasion. Its armament, motorization and equipment make one forget that Germany was in its fifth war year. All the men were specialists, and experts from the Army artillery were assigned as instruction officers.

On June 8, 1944 the batteries marched into their planned firing positions in the Caen area. The 1st Battery used their mortar fire, which had a demoralizing effect on the enemy, to support the action of the 12th SS Armored Division "Hitler Youth" six kilometers northwest of Caen. The impacts of the mortar shells differed greatly from those of normal artillery shells. Thge 17-cm cannons were used chiefly to attack enemy preparation areas. With the help of air artillery, the high range of 30 kilometers was used. For openers, the 3rd Battery sent a heavy hail of fire at the French battle cruiser "Jean Bart" that secured the mouth of the Orne. The 68-kilogram cannon shells hit the ship hard and detonated ammunition on board.

Under heavy fire from enemy ships' guns, Obersturmbannführer Steineck personally directed the unit's fire from an observation post in the Brucourt area. Two landing craft were sunk and several troop transporters were hit. The enemy landing near Riva-Bella was constantly disturbed. Through observed fire, three transport planes could be destroyed on field airstrips. The success of the heavy unit was recognized in an order of the I. SS Armored Corps on June 17, 1944.

According to their role as Corps artillery, the batteries changed their positions at short intervals, in order to have an effect on the focal points of the battles. One other focus of action was the fight for the town and airfield of Carpiquet, the last bulwark of the defensive ring around Caen. For the two 17-cm cannon batteries in particular, it was no problem to provide effective support even at great distances. The hard-fighting "HJ" could always be given support. The advance of a Canadian corps on Falaise was slowed, and a Polish armored division was decimated by the 21-cm mortars. On August 18, 1944 the unit began its withdrawal. Its range allowed it to stay outside the enemy's pincer movements. Within the general withdrawal movements it crossed the Seine toward Belgium. All its guns were brought back!

The fact that the heavy guns could be moved forward, despite enemy air superiority, on the snowy, icy and winding roads of the Ardennes must be regarded as a miracle. Meanwhile the 2nd Battery was rearmed from cannons to 21-cm mortars.

In Hungary, at the Gran bridgehead and the Plattensee, only the two mortar batteries saw action. For want of ammunition, Italian shells of somewhat different calibers also had to be used. Between Varpalota and Veszprem, on the south slope of the Bacony Forest, the mortars went into position to fight against the Russian "steamroller" that had broken through. For the 2nd Battery, only two mortars were still usable. They stood alone in their positions at Tschöss-Puszta. In the night individual infantrymen got away from the battery over an unguarded slope. They reported that there were no longer any German troops before the mouths of the two mortars. The neavy 20-cm guns were unprotected for the first time. A position change would have been advisable to avoid a direct attack and become effective. The Battery Chief instructed the Unit Commander, SS Sturmbannführer Wilhelm Preuss. Preuss immediately stated his case to Arko 1 of the 1st SS Armored Corps. The position change was not allowed. The Corps staff was located in Tesch, very near the battery. The 21-cm mortars were to take over the covering fire for the Corps and cover the withdrawing staff.

Thus on the next morning the two mortars of Obersturmführer Hinrich Garbade were the last ones to face the enemy. When the Soviet tanks, carrying infantrymen, rolled toward the battery, the 21-cm mortars opened fire directly at the leading tanks. The salvo tore the colossus apart like toys. Steel flew through the air like cardboard. Even the tanks that followed were knocked out of the battle. But then the two mortars' fate was sealed. Reloading took much too long. So as not to be overrun and captured, the guns had to be made unusable in the last minute. From then on the Garbade Battery, along with parts of the Staff, saw action only as the "Garbade Infantry Group". On the High Wall near Wiener Neustadt they defended their position from the powerful Soviet elite troops. The 1st Battery fired its last gun at the advancing Soviet Stalin tanks near St. Pölten. At Mariazell the unit gathered for the last time before becoming American prisoners during the night.

IM NAMEN DES FÜHRERS
VERLEIHE ICH
DEM
SS-Obersturmführer
Hinrich Garbade
1./s.SS-Art.Abt. 101
DAS
EISERNE KREUZ
1. KLASSE
K.Gef.St., 7. Juli 1944
Der Kommandierende General
SS-Obergruppenführer und
Panzergeneral der Waffen-SS
(DIENSTGRAD UND DIENSTSTELLUNG)

The award certificate of the Iron Cross I for Ost. Garbade, eventual leader of the Garbade Battle Group.

Glossary of Artillery Concepts from A to Z

Advanced Observer: Young officer or experienced NCO, usually called VB, accompanying riflemen in the infantry, tanks, reconnaissance unit or advance unit, for early artillery support of the attacking troops.

Aiming Gunner: K1, the most important man in the gun crew for aiming in distance and traverse, deputy gun leader.

Ammunition Squad: in the battery, as cannon in the division.

Angles of Elevation: Cannons and howitzers in the lower angles (to 45%), mortars in the higher (above 45%).

Army Artillery: Motorized artillery groups of varied caliber for strengthening, forming focal points, fighting against artillery, special tasks or actions; as of autumn 1944 often gathered in brigades.

Artillery: Originally all war weapons, then firearms, then guns, now so called according to tactical and local use, by trajectory, caliber, mobility and special tasks.

Artillery Commander: Troop leader of the corps artillery and special advisor of the Commanding General of the Army Corps, responsible for the complete command of the artillery, corresponding to higher artillery commanders in the Army.

Artillery Communication Command: Informative and reporting organ under the command of an officer with an assigned battle group for coupling of firing and movement without firing tasks, in unusual cases also an individual officer (AVO).

Artillery Scout Troop: Preparation and information for action of strong units in the hand of the higher command.

Artillery Survey Command: Organ of a unit for calculating firing positions, securing precise firing data, measuring important points in enemy territory with their own calculating position.

Ballistics: Theory of firing, "ballistic achievement", total performance of a shell, air pressure, wind, temperature are values of "ballistic reporting" (BWE), calculated by a battery's reckoning troop, AVT of the unit and regimental weather platoon.

Barrel: The basic barrel and mantle of a gun, with riflings and springs, breech with lock, formerly cast and forged, now drawn and bored, mounted in the gun cradle, secured by the barrel brake and recuperator, with varied lifetime according to charge; very heavy ones are mounted on special barrel carriages.

Battery: Comnmand and personnel unit with 4 to 6 guns, commanded from a battery troop, with fire control by the gun echelon, and led by a battery officer.

Blinding: Tactical concept for using fog to prevent being seen by enemy observers.

Breech: Cover of the loading chamber of a gun, with screw, sliding or cranked lock, by hand, semi- or fully automatic (only for shell amunition).

Bursting Point: Determined by raising the trajectory (clinometer) or changing the burning time of the fuze in the trajectory (double fuze) for ranging, to determine the detonation, and in special cases for effective fire.

Caliber: Stated shot weight, later diameter of the barrel mouth, often including barrel length, for example: L/45 (caliber units).

Call Battery: The battery nearest to the unit's observation post or command post, for quick fire.

Canister Radio: Type b or d for advanced observers as means of communication, with dry cells or wet accumulators, even in heavy frost, carried on the back as sending-and-receiving box and equipment box.

Cannon: Standard name for guns, expecially long-range guns with long barrels, extended trajectory, great penetrating power, for example, 7.5-cm light field cannon, sFK 8 (10 cm), heavy cannons between 17 and 24 cm, railroad cannons for heavy flat fire.

Cartridge: Metal or cardboard drum with propellant charge for the shell, placed in the butt of the barrel.

Charge: Specified parts of the propellant in the cartridge, their choice determining the range, trajectory and impact of the shell.

Clinometer: Aiming device to determine the terrain angle, basic setting and layering, as well as raising of the trajectory.

Command Post: From unit upward to fire control of the group, with best view of the affected areas.

Concentrated Fire: Concentration of fire by several batteries or units on a target area in time and space for strong impact.

Crippling: Tactical concept used in warfare but not officially in peacetime.

Defective Burst: Mistaken disintegration of a shell (weak burst).

Delayed Ignition: Manipulated explosion of shells with ignition set for "delay" from ground to air detonation after the delay, with great splinter effect (at angles of impact up to 29 degrees).

Director: Scope with mount on a horizontal measuring circle with 6400 lines and magnetic needle, for aiming the battery, As R I for the battery position, R II for the firing position, important NCO's task.

Double Fuze: Clockwork or burning fuze installed in addition to an impact fuze, to detonate a shell before the end of its trajectory.

Dud: Fired artillery shell that did not detonate.

Efficaceous Fire: Continued fire against pinpoint targets, otherwise flat fire at effective ranges.

Elevation: According to the battery officer's command to the aiming gunner, to be set on a sight in meters, degrees or lines corresponding to shot range.

Expirator: Misfiring shell that does not break into splinters.

Fire Command: Vocal command with load, type of shell, single gun or whole battery, direction, distance, ammunition, manner of carrying out.

Fire Control: Precisely concentrated fire in terms of time and space, under observation in the unit or regiment to achieve firing superiority according to observation or targeting.

Fire, Order to: To open fire.

Fire Plan: Result of agreement among troop leaders and artillery for opening fire, combined effect, support, length of time, pauses, rate of fire, distribution and direction.

Firing Concepts: For firing and combat tasks: hold down, shoot down, blind.

Firing, forms of: For firing instruction and orders, such as disturbing, destructive, need or barrage fire.

Firing Mission: Tactical command to open fire on worthwhile targets.

Firing Position: Location of guns with security, cover, close defense and places for crew .

Firing, types of: By gun, group of guns, salvo, stratum or surprise attack, with dispersal in length and breadth.

Flash-ranging: Targeting the muzzle flash of enemy guns by measurement to determine position, amplified by sound measurement.

Flash Reducer: Saline substance added to the cartridge to dampen muzzle flash.

Fundamentals of Firing: Definite or not, according to charts and measurements, if necessary determined by one's own fire, as a rule 1:100,000, today 1:50,000.

Gun Carriage or Mount: Whole substructure of the gun, upper and lower mount, construed for field guns as box, spread or cross mount, or fixed as a pivot mount.

Howitzer: Light 10.5- or heavy 15-cm gun with more arched trajectory than a cannon.

Impact Fuze: Sensitive igniter that detonates as soon as it touches the ground; fuze without or with delay for penetrating shells, mines and ricochet effects, impact fuzes with or without delay.

Light Gun: Recoil-free special development, 7.5 and 10.5 cm for normal shells, used by paratroops and in roadless areas.

Limber Position: Place for limbers and tractors, away from the firing position of the gun squad, under command of the master sergeant (Staff Scharführer).

Mortar: Steep-firing gun, effective against cover and fortifications, caliber 21, 30.5, 42 and 60 cm.

Muzzle Brake: Introduced in 1942 to improve the ranges of small calibers.

Muzzle Velocity: Speed of a shell in meters per second as it leaves the gun barrel (Vo) on a presumably unchanged direct course.

Observation: Via main observation post with battery chief and battery troop from advanced observer (VB) for non-visible areas and endangered sectors.

Penetration: For explosive projectiles, it depends on velocity, size, shape; for shells on angle of impact, shape and resisting strength of the shell, design of the shell, delay of ignition.

Planned Firing: Against not observable targets for which zeroing in is impossible, but that must cause surprise, based on definite firing principles.

Position Change: Weak moment of the artillery, only into planned, ordered, located, possibly prepared and measured firing positions.

Ranging: Testing range and direction to a target by visual observation or reconnaissance means with a narrow or wide fork as well as a row, usually with one gun, also at practice and comparison targets.

Ranging Troop: Assigned by the battery leader to work at the reckoning post on firing plans and fire control as well as calculating the BWE with charts or artillery calculators.

Rate of Fire: Succession or cadence of shots with number of shots per minute or hour, depending on the operating crew and its situation, loading process and type of firing, varying for gun types from light howitzer to mortar (6-1 per minute).

Readiness to Fire: Effective readiness at the earliest possible moment in expectation of a fire command or, if ordered, reporting after a command to fire.

Reconnaissance: Most vital prerequisite for artillery effect and its tactical command from systematic eyewitnessing via observation units with light and sound measuring systems, as well as means of observation such as balloons, aviators and observers.

Rifling: right-spiraling grooves to stabilize a shell in flight for better targeting accuracy, by grooves and leading rings for shells, by jets for missiles.

Rolling Barrage: Attack of infantry and automatically proceeding preparatory fire suited to the landscape, by plan (firing plan, time schedule), developed by Bruckmüller in World War I.

Scattering: Intentional firing with varied range and traverse, for locating targets, as opposed to accurate targeting, depending on terrain and barrel wear.

Self-propelled Gun: Transition from wheeled vehicle to tracked vehicle, linked with doubled susceptability as of 1942.

Shell Weight: Influences loading procedure and shot range, as well as transport and supplying, amount of propellant charge needed for effect.

Shot Table: Collection of all technical data for a specific type of gun.

Single Gun: For ranging a battery or unit, also used if necessary for precise targeting in direct aim against bunkers, fortifications or armored vehicles.

Splinter Effect: Breaking of a shell into as small fragments as possible, scattering to front, back and both sides.

Surveying: Calculation by troop survey units or troops, survey battery of a reconnaissance unit and survey unit of the Army.

Taking Position: Between marching and readiness to fire, placing guns in planned and, if possible, measured and prepared positioning areas.

Target: Only "worthwhile" or special target, entered on targeting point cards with group of numerals showing level of command.

Targeting: Direct at a readily visible target, otherwise indirect, as parallel, point or needle procedures to determine the traverse of the guns.

Targeting Devices: For direct and indirect aiming, panoramic scope, telescope as makeshift device, director, shear scope.

Unit (Abteilung): Corresponding to a battalion, the fighting and firing unit of the artillery led by fire control, target advising or combat tasks.

Working Gun: A single gun outside a battery's firing position to disguise it from reconnaissance when zeroing in, for disturbing fire or sending a ballistic weather report.

Zero Line: General direction of aim of a battery at the middle of the ordered area of effect, usually at a fixed point or grid—north on the map, to calculate the traverse with "more" or "less", always set according to the median gun (2nd or 3rd) in the middle of the firing position, also zero point in calculating and commanding activities.

Rank Comparison for Waffen-SS and Army

SS Rank	Army Rank	
Kanonier	Kanonier	
Oberkanonier	Oberkanonier	
Sturmmann	Gefreiter	
Rottenführer	Obergefreiter	Enlisted Men
Unterscharführer	Unteroffizier	
Scharführer *	Unterfeldwebel	
Standartenjunker	Fähnrich	
Oberscharführer	Feldwebel	
Hauptscharführer	Oberfeldwebel	
Standartenoberjunker	Oberfähnrich	
Sturmscharführer *	Stabsfeldwebel	Non-commissioned Officers
Untersturmführer	Leutnant	
Obersturmführer	Oberleutnant	
Hauptsturmführer	Hauptmann	
Sturmbannführer	Major	
Obersturmbannführer	Oberstleutnant	
Standartenführer	Oberst	
Oberführer	Oberst	Officers
Brigadeführer	Generalmajor	
Gruppenführer	Generalleutnant	
Obergruppenführer	General der Artillerie, etc.	
Oberstgruppenführer *	Generaloberst	Generals

The ranks of SS Scharführer and SS Sturmscharführer were dropped during the war. As of 1942 the rank of SS Oberstgruppenführer was introduced. Sepp Dietrich and Paul Hausser were the only holders of this rank in the Waffen-SS.

Service of the Artillery Regiment of the Leibstandarte SS Adolf Hitler, since 10/22/1943 officially called SS Armored Artillery Regiment 1 "LSSAH" of the 1st SS Armored Division "LSSAH":

1940 August-December	Establishment of the regiment in Wappingen near Metz, presentation of the "Führer's Standard" amd Christmas celebration with Adolf Hitler on 12/26/1940 in the Bergamt in Metz.
1941 January-March April	Departure to Romania of the advance command under Ostubaf. Staudinger. Action in the Tulcea area, transport from Metz to Campulung, march into Bulgaria, attack on Yugoslavia, crossing the Greek border, advance on Klidi, combat around the Klisura Pass, artillery battle on Kastoria Lake on 4/15/41, crossing the Aliakmon near Grevena, advance southward to the Gulf of Patras, securing around Navpaktos as of 4/26/41. participation of the 3rd and 4th Batteries in the victory parade in Athens of 5/3/41, transfer to Larissa.
June	Wischau troop training camp.
July	March into Soviet Union, combat on North Road, defensive combat around Kiev.
August	Closing the ring around Uman, combat at Sasselye, taking of Cherson.
September-October	Refreshing in Bobrinez, advance to Crimea, breakthrough combat at Perekop and Armyansk, advance at Melitopol, taking of Berdyansk and Mariupol. Combat at the Mius crossing before Taganrog and duel with armored trains, capture of Taganrog, combat east of the Mius, advance on Rostov, street fighting in Rostov, relocation and winter quarters on the Ssambek.
1942 June	Positional war
July	Coastal defense on Sea of Azov, transfer to Stalino, rail transport to France, participation in the great field parade of the LSSAH in Paris on 7/29/42.
August-December	Visit of Commanding General of the 15th Army, Generaloberst Haase, display of the 1st Battery, alarming after Canadian landing near Dieppe.
(December)	Refreshing.
1943 January-February March	Transport to the east, defensive combat on the Donetz on both sides ofChuguyev, combat east of Kharkov, defensive combat at Rogan depot, evacuation of Kharkov, attack on Bereka, defensive combat south of Kharkov, at Yeremeyeva and pocket combat at Yefremovka, advance northward over the Msha sectorm advance on Kharkov from north, combat at Alexeyevka, street fighting in Kharkov, taking of "Red Square", conquest of Belgorod.
July	Beginning of Operation "Citadel," advance on Yakovlevo, combat at Luchki, tank battle at Prokhorovka on 7/12/43. holding the attained lines.
August-October	Transfer via Innsbruck to Italy, disarming the Italian army in northern Italy. Action in Yugoslavian partisan area near Gortz-Laibach-Trieste.
November December	Rail transport to Ukraine, gathering around Belaya Zerkov, combat at Shitomir, Brusilov, Radomyshl and Chepovici, defensive combat at Berdichev, combat at the sugar factory, transport over the Guiva.
1944 January-February	Action around Yanushpol, attack on Krasnopol, counterattack northeast of Vinniza, pocket combat at Gaissin and Lipovez, relief combat to break the pocket of Cherkassy-Korsun to Lyssianka, transfer to Proskurov.
March April	Combat east of Ternopol near Manachin and Kupel, action of artillery battle groups in Hube pocket, defense before Losiacz, withdrawal combat via Ulaskovce to Buczacz, rail transport via Lemberg to Mol, Belgium, reorganization of the regiment.
June-July	Transfer to the invasion front, defensive combat west and south of Caen, at Carpiquet, Bully, Bras, Houbert, Soliers, attack toward Avranches.
August	Break out of the pocket of Falaise, withdrawal combat over the Seine to Belgium.
September-November	Refreshing in Westphalia.
December	Beginning of the Ardennes offensive, combat around Stavelot and La Gleize, transfer southward, action at Bastogne, withdrawal from the front around Bastogne, transfer via St. Vith to Cologne and Bonn.
1945 January	Transport to the Raab area in Hungary.
February March	Participation in Operation "Southwind," attack on the Gran bridgehead and "Spring's Awakening"—Plattensee offensive, withdrawal combat from Varpalota to western Hungary, defense at Neusideler See, combat in direction of Wiener Neustadt.
April-May	Withdrawal into the Vienna Woods, final combat south of St. Pölten, capitulation.

The regiment was on the western front twice (invasion and Ardennes offensive), and twice in the Southeast (Balkan campaign and Italian action). Five large-scale actions in all took place on the eastern front. The Red Army was always in the enemy's southern sector.

The soldiers of the Leibstandarte SS Adolf Hitler wore, besides the "Adolf Hitler" sleeve stripe on the left forearm, the script LAH letters on the shoulder patches. Beling allowed to belong to this unique troop was the greatest recognition for each man. Photo: VB Rothe

Waffen-SS Commanders

Mark C. Yerger

The units of the Waffen-SS were some of the most successful and influential combat formations produced by any country in this century. Their abilities and accomplishments, in both defense and offense, remain legendary. Finally, the commanders of these elite units are examined here in detail.

The Army, Corps and Division Leaders of a Legend-Augsberger to Kreutz

Volume I contains forty-four biographies that reveal the lives of the most senior Waffen-SS commanders.
Size: 8 1/2" x 11" ■ over 400 b/w photographs, maps, documents ■ 352 pp.
ISBN: 0-7643-0356-2 ■ hard cover ■ $59.95

The Army, Corps and Divisional Leaders of a Legend – Krüger to Zimmermann

Volume II contains 61 biographies that reveal the lives of the most senior Waffen-SS commanders. Details are provided for education, as well as pre-Third Reich era service in military and civil posts, and includes promotions, assignments and decorations. The 1933-1945 era (the most detailed) reveals all their commands and related data similar to their earlier service. Includes an addendum to Vol. 1 that adds both text and photographic material uncovered during the concluding research.
Size: 8 1/2" x 11" ■ over 440 b/w photographs, 25 documents, glossary, appendix, index ■ 392 pp.
ISBN: 0-7643-0769-X ■ hard cover ■ $59.95